PRACTICAL TRAINING

How to Introduce Target Setting

A Guide for Trainers and Managers

RICHARD HALE

KOGAN PAGE
Published in association with the
Institute of Training and Development

TO OLIVER

First published in 1993

Apart from any fair dealing for the purposes of research or private study, or criticism or review, as permitted under the Copyright, Designs and Patents Act, 1988, this publication may only be reproduced, stored or transmitted, in any form or by any means, with the prior permission in writing of the publishers, or in the case of reprographic reproduction in accordance with the terms of licences issued by the Copyright Licensing Agency. Enquiries concerning reproduction outside those terms should be sent to the publishers at the undermentioned address:

Kogan Page Limited
120 Pentonville Road
London N1 9JN

© Richard Hale, 1993

British Library Cataloguing in Publication Data

A CIP record for this book is available from the British Library.

ISBN 0 7494 0959 2

Typeset by Koinonia Ltd, Bury
Printed and bound in Great Britain by Biddles Ltd,
Guildford and King's Lynn

Contents

Series Editor's Foreword   *Roger Buckley*   9

Introduction   11

I

THE CONTEXT OF TARGET SETTING

1 Target Setting in Context   15
Targets and the Corporate Environment *15*
Moving Training Back to the Workplace *17*
Using Targets for Direction and Motivation *18*
The Role of the Trainer in Target Setting *19*
… and Assessment *21*

2 The Emergence of Performance Management   23
The Purpose of Performance Appraisal *24*
History and Trends *27* Performance Management *30*
Case Study – The Potential Pitfalls of Performance Appraisal *31*

3 Integrating Target Setting with Existing Systems   35
Reward and Remuneration Systems *36* Competencies *38*
Training and Development Programmes *40*
Total Quality Management *41*

4 Preparing the Organization for Success through Target Setting   46
Time Constraints *47* Seniority *49*
Administrative and Service Functions *51*
Targets for Technical Roles *55*
Not Everyone wants to be Promoted –
Not Everyone will be Promoted *59*

II
THE PRACTICE OF TARGET SETTING

5 Target Setting in Practice 63
What are Targets? *64* Quantitative Targets *65*
Developmental Targets *66* Success Criteria *67*
Top-down Support – Bottom-up Development *68*
Reinforcing Organizational Messages *69*
Using Targets to Breed Success *70*

6 Target Setting and Review 74
Preparation for Review when Targets are Set *75*
Balancing Targets with Other Responsibilities *77*
Encouraging Self Review and Continual Review *80*
Timescales from Target Setting to Review *81*

7 The Interpersonal Skills of Target Setting and Review 86
Communication Skills *87* Listening *89* Questioning *92*
Feedback *93* Confrontation *93* Perceptual Distortions *94*

III
TRAINING IN TARGET SETTING AND TARGET ACHIEVEMENT

8 Training Managers and Employees to Set Targets 99
Model for an On-site Target Setting Workshop *101*
Model for an Off-job Residential Training Course *102*

9 How to Achieve Targets through Visualization 106
Self-fulfilling Prophecy *106* Visualization *107*

APPENDIX 1
Higgins and Duke Case Study – Possible Answers 109

APPENDIX 2
Handouts for Target Setting Training 111

APPENDIX 3
Example Targets 116

APPENDIX 4
Reference list of Relevant Videos 120

References 121

Index 123

Series Editor's Foreword

Organizations get things done when people do their jobs effectively. To make this happen they need to be well trained. A number of people are likely to be involved in this training: identifying the needs of the organization and of the individual, selecting or designing appropriate training to meet those needs, delivering it and assessing how effective it was. It is not only 'professional' or full-time trainers who are involved in this process; personnel managers, line managers, supervisors and job holders are all likely to have a part to play.

This series has been written for all those who get involved with training in some way or another, whether they are senior personnel managers trying to link the goals of the organization with training needs or job holders who have been given responsibility for training newcomers. Therefore, the series is essentially a practical one which focuses on specific aspects of the training function. This is not to say that the theoretical underpinnings of the practical aspects of training are unimportant. Anyone seriously interested in training is strongly encouraged to look beyond 'what to do' and 'how to do it' and to delve into the areas of why things are done in a particular way. The series has become so popular that it is intended to include additional volumes whenever a need is found for practical guidelines in some area of training.

The authors have been selected because they have considerable practical experience. All have shared, at some time, the same difficulties, frustrations and satisfactions of being involved in training and are now in a position to share with others some helpful and practical guidelines.

In this book Richard Hale looks at an area which has taken on a high profile in the recession-hit nineties, namely target setting. Organizations of all kinds have been forced to examine the ways in which they operate. Many are introducing major cultural change programmes in order to survive and to be competitive in a rapidly changing business environment. Such programmes place considerable emphasis on individual contribution and accountability. This means setting targets. As agents for change, trainers acting as internal consultants should be at the heart of the process. The contents of this book provide both trainers and line managers with sound knowledge and guidelines to introduce a system of target setting and appraisal and to put in place a training programme for the benefit of all participants.

ROGER BUCKLEY

Introduction

Whether they are known as goals, targets or objectives, individuals and organizations are constantly seeking ways of achieving them. For individuals it is often a case of setting personal targets which will lead to personal and career development in a particular direction; for an organization, target setting is seen as a means of helping all employees to pull in the same direction with a view to gaining competitive advantage.

Target setting provides the vehicle for the achievement of individual ambitions and dreams and for organizational competitiveness. All too often, however, the cry is heard that 'we cannot set targets because our job is different'.

In this book a number of clear guidelines are given on how to set targets in all functions of business and in all sectors. These guidelines are supported by many real examples of targets taken from organizations which the author has worked with. For the trainer, the human resource professional or indeed the line manager with training responsibility this is a practical guide on how to establish target setting and how to anticipate and work with the natural concerns which employees will have.

Part I considers major developments in how targets have been established and reviewed in organizations and in particular the emergence of the concept of performance management. It is explained that for target setting to be successfully implemented at an organizational level there needs to be astute recognition of cultural and historical factors. Some examples of how target setting relates to other organizational initiatives are worked through in Chapter 3 with the aim of demonstrating how such connections need to be made depending on the circumstances of the organization.

In Part II the practicality of target setting and review and the associated interpersonal skills are explored. In setting up a target setting initiative the trainer needs to design and deliver effective training; this might take several forms and some examples of training programmes are shown in Part III.

Target Setting

Finally some recent research on how we actually achieve goals is considered. This includes the concept of imagery and visualization whereby individuals create pictures of successful outcomes, and through a process of mental rehearsal, can achieve their personal targets.

I

The Context of Target Setting

1 Target Setting in Context

> SUMMARY <

In this chapter we consider the context of target setting and why it is particularly appropriate as an approach in the light of important trends in training and development. In particular we consider the following factors and developments:

- pressures on the corporate environment mean that change is the norm;
- methods of training have developed significantly in recent years;
- training and development have moved back to the workplace;
- targets can provide direction and motivation for employees;
- targets can establish consistency across the organization;
- the key player in implementing target setting is the trainer.

The trainer should be aware of these overall developments and trends. Such awareness will provide breadth of thinking when considering how to implement target setting in the trainer's organization.

Targets and the Corporate Environment

In recent years the corporate environment has seen dramatic change and it is likely that the only constant for organizations in the future will, in fact, be change. This applies equally to the production and service environment and to the private and public sector.

Key trends have been:

- increased competition;
- shrinking markets;
- collaboration with competitors, customers and suppliers;

The Context of Target Setting

- higher customer expectations in terms of quality and service;
- a more fluid and demanding labour market;
- advancing technolgy;
- diminishing resources.

The pressures on all employees to do more with less have never been greater and the more astute managers are realizing that it is better to focus on doing the right things rather than simply 'doing things right'.

The following generic skills and abilities have now come to the fore. These skills are applicable in a range of situations rather than specific to any one job:

- teamworking;
- building relationships;
- interpersonal skills;
- persuasion and influence;
- knowing how to do things rather than just what to do;
- learning to learn;
- networking;
- being entrepreneurial;
- processing information;
- coping with change;
- problem solving and decision making;
- creativity.

Sometimes such skills are viewed as 'soft' or immeasurable. As a result, their development tends to be neglected and they are often avoided when it comes to setting targets. It is, however, just as possible to set real targets for these subjects as it is in the 'hard' or seemingly more tangible areas. Of course it is more difficult than setting, for instance, a production or sales target, but with a sound set of techniques and with the right spirit of implementation it is possible to set targets for *any* job. After all if you do not know where you are going the chances are you will end up in the wrong place!

The key to surviving and potentially thriving in this dynamic corporate environment is for employees to understand what is expected of them and actually to have a say in determining the main targets for their job. They then need plenty of help and encouragement in working towards targets so that they are successfully achieved.

There needs to be open recognition from the organization of such success, even joint celebration within the workplace, followed by negotiation of new targets covering new issues. The whole process becomes forward looking – a way of helping the organization and the individual move successfully into the future. And if the focus is on success rather than failure the process also becomes self-perpetuating – success breeds success. So motivated by the successful achievement of personal targets and the recognition this brings employees will be hungry to agree the next set of targets for the future.

Moving Training Back to the Workplace

Traditionally we have trained people in job specific skills such as sales, engineering, finance etc. and if they have shown the ability and inclination for management we may have offered management training. Management training in less enlightened organizations has invariably been made available after promotion rather than in preparation for the next move up; thus the major thrust of the training in such circumstances has been remedial: aiming to correct a deficiency or weakness rather than truly developmental. Unfortunately this is often how candidates also view the offer of training; it may be interpreted as an overt or implied criticism. How often have you heard staff brag that they have been selected for training? In organizations such as these it has been the sort of subject that has been whispered about almost apologetically.

Many organizations have survived with this approach to developing people largely because their structures are functional with little need to work across disciplines; each department working away in splendid isolation and only coming together through the coordinating efforts of the general manager. Of paramount importance in this scenario is gaining functional skills which will equip the person for life, if they are lucky.

Increasingly, however, organizations are realizing the importance of communication across functions and teamworking. In other words business structures are regrouping with the main uniting factor being the customer or client rather than the department or the organization chart. Additionally the job-specific skills of yesterday and today will not necessarily be those of tomorrow; therefore it is becoming more important to enable employees to cope with changing demands and the need to be flexible, rather than to provide a set of specific skills which will last for life.

The other major change in the training world has been the diversification in the range of options now available as ways of training people. Historically there have been three types of training on offer with little variation available for those who did not really fit into one of the following categories:

- initial skills training – usually in the form of a time-serving apprenticeship for school leavers;
- professional training – usually for those who had progressed academically beyond secondary education; and
- off-job training courses – for those in industry unable to spend too long away from their place of work.

Increasingly, however, training has become recognized as something which should be continuous. The notion of skills has broadened and is constantly changing as technology develops; it is no longer possible to rely on initial or professional training given during the early part of an employee's career.

The ways of being trained are now many and varied. There is open or distance learning with multimedia methods and an emphasis on self-study; this might include workbooks, videotapes, computer-based training or interactive video. There is total flexibility regarding the time and place of study which offers the opportunity for a balance to be struck between the use of work time and the employee investing some of his or her own time. There is work-based coaching, secondment and mentoring. These all represent approaches to developing people which bring training much closer to the workplace.

There is much less emphasis on the classroom as the only environment for learning, and if we do decide to move away from the job for training, methods have shifted thankfully away from the 'chalk and talk' approach to more active 'hands-on' or experiential techniques of learning. The other major development in recent years is the advent of the competency movement. It is now possible to gain qualifications by demonstrating ability in the job situation; an excellent example of the working environment taking centre stage in the development process.

Target setting, if implemented professionally, also provides an opportunity to link development of skills and knowledge directly to the specific jobs of employees. By discussing and agreeing areas of priority for further attention it is possible to provide a framework for continuous improvement. If backed up by guidance and support both on and off the job, the individual will develop personally and be able to offer a higher level of contribution to the success of the business.

Using Targets for Direction and Motivation

So target setting fits in with the movement of training and development away from the more academic and off-job situation towards the workplace and the needs of the individual. Targets can give direction to employees as well as a means of coping with the pressures of change. They can help the development of individual skills and can prove highly motivational: if they do relate to individual needs the process will have a high degree of validity and relevance in the eyes of the employee.

If pitched at the appropriate level for the individual they will provide 'stretch' which means that employees will realize that they do have capabilities beyond their current repertoire of skills and will be more motivated to achieve their full potential.

At the same time they can help at an organizational level to reinforce key messages about the culture and expected standards of work and behaviour. This does not mean producing an organization of automatons, because it is important to include targets which are specific to the development of the individual. Targets do, though, provide a means of establishing consistency in areas which have been identified as important to the values of the organization. This might, for instance, be to do with the image presented to customers, care for the environment, methods of communication, decision making or formality and informality. The scope for reinforcing corporate values is enormous and targets can help pull a group of individuals together and face them in the same direction while drawing strength from individual abilities.

For any target setting initiative to succeed there needs to be top-level support and involvement. For anyone attempting to implement a target setting initiative one of the most difficult objections to deal with is 'I cannot set targets for my staff because my manager will not set targets for me.' Clearly there needs to be demonstrable involvement from the highest level down – and yes, you can set targets for directors and chief executives. Simply paying lip service to target setting is not enough; there needs to be an initial drive to set up a system which will involve professional and participative training in how to set targets followed by ongoing coaching and guidance.

The Role of the Trainer in Target Setting

The role of the trainer in all this is vital. First, in the early stages of introduction the trainer will need to devote much energy and persuasive ability to gaining senior level support and involvement. Professionalism and agile strategic thinking is required in identifying the links with – or distinctions from – existing initiatives such as performance appraisal and remuneration systems. Sensitivity to the culture and history of the organization is called for. Resilience is needed in dealing with the inevitable objections and fears.

For those who have seen organizational initiatives come and go before there may be a degree of cynicism: the 'We've seen it all before' syndrome. Such attitudes need to be anticipated and confronted with empathy. There will be some who fear that target setting heralds the advent of 'Big Brother' and that everything they do is being closely monitored and measured. These views must be negated by creating a healthy climate for the implementation of target setting where everyone feels that they stand to gain personally in some way from the process. Then there are the spurious reasons for not being able to set targets 'here' because:

'we operate in a constantly changing environment',
'we have too many day–to-day pressures and interruptions',
'we are too technical',
'we are too creative – we work on inspiration',
'we are too senior for targets to be set at this level', or
'we provide an administrative service so we cannot work to targets'.

What all these objections signal is not the fact that it is impossible to set targets but that there is likely to be a lot of apprehension when the subject is first raised and that people have never been properly trained in setting targets.

Having laid the ground for the introduction of target setting and created the right spirit for cooperation and successful implementation, the trainer must demonstrate the core skills of training programme design, marketing and implementation. Any training programme needs to deal with both the practical considerations of the target setting initiative (such as documentation and implementation strategy) and the development of target setting skills.

The trainer should involve staff at all levels who are involved in target setting – either setting targets for others or having targets set for themselves. During training, delegates need to be able to practise drawing up targets using the ground rules and techniques they have learned.

Like most organizational initiatives it is not sufficient to deliver the training and just leave it to happen: with this approach it will wither and die. There is an instrumental role for the trainer in giving ongoing support and guidance to employees at all levels. This will include further practical guidance for some and simply cajoling and lots of encouragement for others.

Once targets have become accepted as an integral part of management and a motivational tool it makes most sense to spread best practice throughout the organization, and who is in a better position to do this than the trainer?

Target Setting in Context

Human Resource Function	**Senior Management**
• Overseeing the initiative • Giving/obtaining specialist advice • Administration • Documentation • Moderation of assessment • Linking to other HR systems	• Gaining agreement to introduce it • Selling the concept to senior management • Getting support to help sell it downwards • Active involvement and participation

THE TRAINER

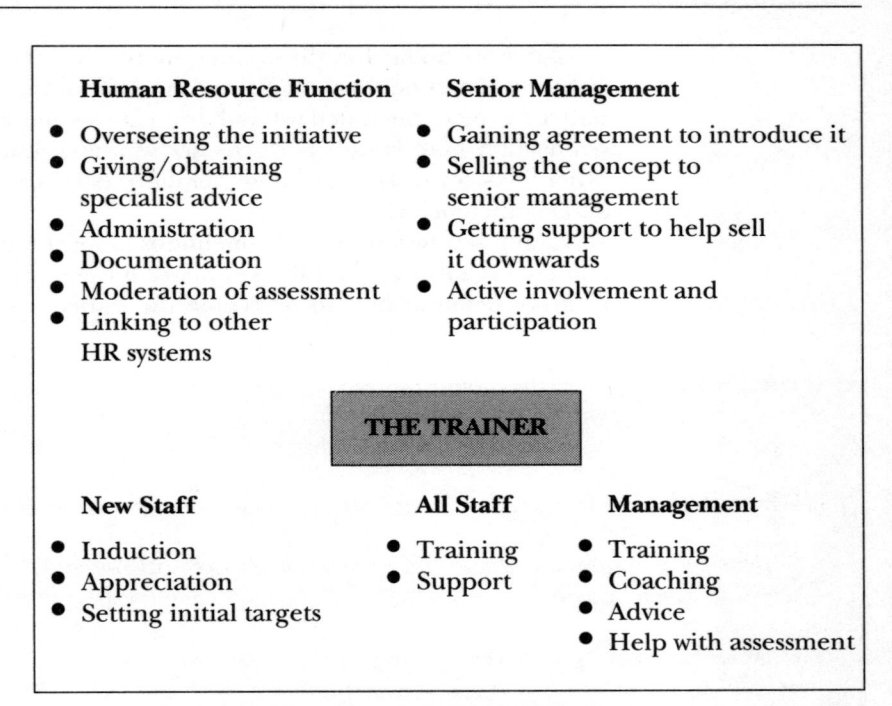

New Staff	**All Staff**	**Management**
• Induction • Appreciation • Setting initial targets	• Training • Support	• Training • Coaching • Advice • Help with assessment

Figure 1.1 *Target setting – the role of the trainer*

... and Assessment

Assessment is always one of the most contentious and emotional aspects of the target setting process. If, however, target setting is implemented effectively then it should be the most trouble-free aspect of all. This will depend on the trainer ensuring that effective targets with built-in success criteria are agreed at the outset. Also it will be essential to ensure that there is open and ongoing dialogue regarding progress towards targets; in this way there are less likely to be surprises at the review stage. The review discussion will then focus on recognizing and summarizing what was achieved and why and offering support for continued development.

As can be seen from Figure 1.1 the trainer has to operate at various levels throughout the organization to ensure the success of any target setting initiative. There are the senior level interfaces where the aim is to gain support and help in selling the concept more widely. This will mean persuading the most senior employees to 'practise what they preach' and work to targets themselves and set targets for their direct reports.

The Context of Target Setting

Closer to home for the trainer there are many parts the human resource department has to play, the most important being to ensure that target setting is integrated with other initiatives and systems. The obvious connection here is with performance appraisal but there may well be other links, for instance, to remuneration systems, training programmes and competencies.

Target setting presents tremendous opportunities for individuals and the organization and the key player is the trainer. We will now look in more detail at how to overcome the difficulties and maximize the benefits.

ACTIVITY

What are the major economic, social and political pressures on your organization?

What are the major changes your organization is currently undergoing or is likely to see in the near future?

How is the organization responding to these pressures and changes in terms of preparing managers and employees to deal with them?

To what extent do employees work to targets?

2 The Emergence of Performance Management

> SUMMARY
>
> In this chapter we consider target setting in the context of performance appraisal and the concept of 'performance management'. In particular we will focus on:
>
> - the purpose of performance appraisal as a motivational tool and to provide valuable organizational information;
> - developments in performance appraisal including the movement towards joint problem solving, focusing on results and the involvement of employees at all levels;
> - important lessons from research on performance management.
>
> Trainers need to be sensitive to whether they are operating in a 'performance management' organization and should identify the relationship between target setting and other performance-related strategies such as performance appraisal and performance-related pay.
>
> We conclude with a case study of performance appraisal which demonstrates some of the potential pitfalls of poor implementation.

Rarely does a target-setting initiative exist in isolation in an organization: the target-setting approach and associated thinking is integrated with or at least linked to wider organizational systems.

The most usual and obvious link is with performance appraisal and the connection of target setting with performance appraisal is covered specifically in this chapter. In the next chapter we consider the links with other organizational initiatives and human resource systems, some of which will be deliberate and carefully contrived and others of which will be more tenuous but no less important and worthy of consideration.

Performance appraisal schemes take various forms depending on the history of appraisal in different organizations and on the style considered most appropriate. This will depend on such factors as sector, culture and job functions. There have been major developments in the field of performance appraisal in recent years and we will track these trends later in this chapter, but first it is worth stepping back and asking the fundamental but often neglected question 'What is the purpose of performance appraisal?'

The Purpose of Performance Appraisal

Essentially the primary purpose of effective performance apppraisal schemes complement precisely the aims of target setting and as such it is most sensible to contextualize target setting within performance appraisal. As mentioned in Chapter 1 in relation to target setting, effective performance appraisal serves the purpose of enhancing the performance of both the organization and the individual. Realistically not all performance appraisal schemes actually achieve this; we will consider the reasons for this later on. In its worst form, for example, performance appraisal can have the effect of demotivating employees and generally lowering morale throughout the organization. Marginally better than schemes which have this effect are performance appraisal schemes which offer benefits and motivation to those who buy into the whole approach but neglect those who do not. Appropriately designed and carefully implemented performance appraisal schemes, however, offer massive potential at both the organizational and individual level.

Properly implemented performance appraisal should open up the opportunity for a healthy two-way discussion between manager and subordinate of performance over a recent period, and make plans for improving performance and developing the individual in the future. This forward looking focus is where target setting plays a major part and a key trend in recent years has been the evolution of this active and dynamic aspect of performance appraisal as opposed to the historic type of scheme which dwelt mainly on the past and static analysis of previous performance. The benefits of the forward focused approach are potentially more motivational. Peters and Waterman (1982) have developed our thinking on the subject of motivation through their research into successful organizations publicized in *In Search of Excellence*; they identified the following basic needs which employees have in organizations and which excellent companies recognize:

- people's need for meaning;
- people's need for some control;
- people's need for positive reinforcement – to believe they are winners.

It was also explained that:

- Actions and behaviours shape attitudes and beliefs, meaning that a powerful way to influence employees is for managers to act in the way they would expect their employees to act.

As shown in Figure 2.1 there is clearly the possibility of satisfying all these needs through effective discussion of performance and planning.

Peters and Waterman Factors	How Performance Appraisal can Satisfy These Needs
Need for meaning	Clear linking of individual jobs with the objectives of the organization
Need for control	Joint discussion between subordinate and manager regarding future job priorities and targets
Need for positive reinforcement	Provision of effective feedback from manager to subordinate
Actions shape attitudes and beliefs	Performance appraisal as the starting point for deciding future action which entails senior-level commitment to help the individual develop

Figure 2.1 *Performance appraisal as a tool for motivation*

By motivating individuals through effective performance appraisal and target setting the ensuing enthusiasm is likely to have an infectious and synergystic influence on others; this multiplier effect will lead to benefits at sectional, departmental and ultimately organizational level.

You may be thinking that this is fine for those who are successful in the performance appraisal interview but for the employee who is on the receiving end of a poor appraisal the effect is more likely to be one of demotivation rather than inspiration. In the case of unprofessionally implemented performance appraisal the effects could indeed include demotivation and feelings of low self esteem, disgruntlement, unfair treatment, victimization and weakness. This does not mean that the less easy issues to discuss, such as areas for improvement or development, should be avoided in order for performance appraisal to motivate. If dealt with skilfully by the appraiser these issues can be discussed objectively and in a positive way with the emphasis on guidance regarding future action and support which will be made available to help the individual hone existing skills and develop in the new areas. It is quite possible for the employee to leave the performance appraisal interview highly motivated by the fact that those niggling worries about possible weaknesses or areas of vulnerability have at last been discussed openly and that there is an offer of future support.

By discussing both strengths and weaknesses of individuals through the performance appraisal interview it is possible for managers and professional trainers to audit continually and systematically the knowledge and skill resources available in a manager's domain. The benefits of this quality of information are many and can help with, for instance, work planning, succession planning and generally improving the likelihood of being able to anticipate future problems and priorities, rather than being pushed into a fire-fighting mode of crisis management.

Finally one of the key aims of many successful performance appraisal schemes is systematically to identify training and development needs. In forward thinking organizations the concept of training does not simply mean an off-job training course for remedial purposes but could include many other options in terms of method of delivery and duration: a number of examples are provided in the checklist in Figure 2.2.

- On-job training
- Further and higher education programmes
- Mentoring
- Coaching
- Secondment
- Sabbatical
- Job rotation
- Self development
- Open learning
- Teach-ins and workshops
- Job enrichment

Figure 2.2 *Performance appraisal and the identification of training needs – methods of training and development*

Performance appraisal can serve many purposes, the most important being motivation of individuals, the maintenance of morale, the identification of strengths and weaknesses throughout the department and the systematic identification of training needs. The principle underpinning all schemes, whatever their design, is to remove subjectivity which is more likely to exist in appraisal without a consistent system or scheme. Having considered the overall aims of appraisal it is instructive to track the trends in the design of performance appraisal schemes and how these relate to the increasing emphasis on target setting.

History and Trends

The last 40 years have seen many changes in the development of performance appraisal but the most significant changes have occurred only recently. This implies that there is no panacea for the ills of previous initiatives, but certainly these changes constitute major advances and certain common factors have emerged which distinguish successful schemes from those fraught with problems. The underlying theme has been the emergence of individual target setting linked to organizational goals and we will show how this principle links to many of the other recent developments.

From Traits to Results-based Assessment

From the mid-twentieth century there was a growth in systematic approaches to appraising performance. Until the mid-1980s the emphasis in most schemes was placed on making judgements about employees against broadly defined traits and behaviours such as:

- Cooperation
- Leadership
- Teamwork
- Initiative
- Attendance and timekeeping
- Diligence
- Interest shown
- Presentation and appearance.

Often the same traits were used throughout the whole organization and assessment was a case of making fairly broad judgements in terms of categories such as excellent, good, room for improvement and poor. In the 1960s this approach was refined into the more systematic 'management by objectives' approach which attempted to apply a much more rigid methodology to quantifying the assessment of performance. Eventually this advanced and more scientific approach to performance appraisal became in many cases self defeating. One of the problems experienced with such schemes was that as the documentation became more complex and onerous for the appraiser, it took on more significance than the actual process of generating healthy dialogue regarding performance. As performamance appraisal systems became more and more complex, in some cases the objective of the appraisee was to beat the system and negotiate the highest rating possible.

With the more forward focused appraisal schemes, assessment tends to relate to the achievement of results and outputs linked to targets which were negotiated at the previous performance appraisal interview. Then, of course, there is the negotiation of new targets to work towards in the future. The targets-based approach, in comparison to the traits-based approach, places the emphasis on the achievement of results which are relevant to the needs of the individuals and their departments rather than making broad judgements against supposedly generic traits. A word of caution here; many management by objectives schemes failed because of the absence of links with the overall aims of the business.

From Input Measurement to Output Measurement

The move towards results-based systems has meant that the method of assessment has moved from attempting to measure the effort or input provided by employees to measuring results or output. Examples of input and output measurements are shown in Figure 2.3.

Inputs	Outputs
Effort	Sound decisions
Concentration	Accuracy
Attendance/Punctuality	Quality of work
Efficiency	Effectiveness
Attitude	Results achieved through others
Interest in job	Application of knowledge
Confidence	Application of skills
Enthusiasm	Problems solved
Self organization	Innovations achieved
Image	Targets met
Drive	Financial performance

Figure 2.3 *Input and output measurements*

Logically, to assess the effectiveness in a particular job role it is essential to focus on outputs despite the natural tendency to consider some of the items shown as inputs as more relevant. This is covered in greater detail in Chapter 5 in relation to the target setting process in practice. A key role for the trainer here is to develop, amongst users of the appraisal system – both appraisers and appraisees – an awareness of the subtle difference between outputs and inputs. The trainer should be continually checking and challenging the targets produced by line management as a means of developing effective target-setting skills.

From Judgemental to Joint Problem Solving

Traditionally the process of appraisal entailed the manager completing relevant documentation, often under pressure from the personnel department, behind closed doors. The appraisal interview consisted of, at best, a run through of the judgements made with no room for input or discussion by the appraisee and some advice on 'how to do better next time'. In even more outmoded examples of performance appraisal the appraisee would not even see or discuss the judgements made with the appraiser and no discussion would take place on areas of success or how to improve.

Increasingly, however, it has been accepted that the most appropriate positioning of performance appraisal should be as a mature discussion of performance with the emphasis on jointly identifying and solving problems relating to performance as well as summarizing, recognizing and even celebrating areas of success and achievement. In fact the more effective managers will continually appraise employees and provide ongoing feedback and support, if only on a less formal basis, and then summarize more formally at the performance appraisal interview. With this approach there are no major surprises for the employee at the performance appraisal interview and the stress and emotional charge is negated leaving the way clear for a frank and healthy two-way discussion.

From Managerial to All Jobs

As it has become increasingly accepted that performance can and indeed should be measured in any job role so the practice of performance appraisal has spread from being the preserve of management jobs to being accepted as a legitimate approach at all levels of the organization in all functions and across business sectors. In Chapter 4 we show specifically how target setting can be applied in all kinds of job role and at all levels.

So the key trends in performance appraisal have been a move away from overly general assessments against stated, but in effect arbitrary criteria and away from the more sophisticated but overspecific mechanical merit-rating systems. The most beneficial systems focus on individual targets which can be realistically assessed through collaborative problem solving and supportive discussion. Locke and Latham (1990) present evidence that goal setting is a major characteristic of appraisals that are effective in bringing about behaviour change.

Progressive organizations have made clear the relationship between improving the performance of the individual and meeting organizational objectives. This is the key tenet behind the movement which has become known as performance management.

Performance Management

Performance management describes the approach many organizations are taking to link individual targets to those of the organization as a whole; rather than operating as a specific technique it is more of a philosophy which potentially incorporates methods such as performance

---

- Performance management organizations were likely to express performance targets in terms of measurable outputs, accountabilities and training or learning targets.
- More success was likely in organizations stressing the importance of ensuring human resource development activities and relating these to the needs of the organization rather than those where the remuneration dimension dominated performance management.
- The challenge for the personnel function is to facilitate the ownership of performance management by line management.
- Organizations implementing performance management systems should consider extrinsic needs of employees such as reward packages and intrinsic needs in terms of personal growth.
- Training and development can be important motivators particularly if linked to career development.

Figure 2.4 *Findings from 'Performance management in the UK – an analysis of the issues' (IPM, 1992. Reproduced by permission of the publishers, The Institute of Personnel Management, IPM House, 35 Camp Road, London SW19 4UX)*

The Emergence of Performance Management

- Mission statement
- Business planning
- Training planning
- Performance appraisal
- Culture change initiatives
- Competencies
- Performance-related pay
- Job evaluation
- Communications initiatives
- Continuous improvement programmes
- Quality circles
- Succession planning
- Target setting:
    Individual/Sectional/Departmental

Figure 2.5 *Management techniques and approaches relating to performance management*

appraisal and performance-related pay. In a study of performance management in the UK, the Institute of Personnel Management (IPM, 1992) found that just under 20 per cent of responding organizations claimed to operate performance management systems. There were some important findings from this study with implications for the success of target setting initiatives. These are summarized in Figure 2.4.

As the number of management techniques has grown, including for example appraisal, job evaluation and performance related pay, they have frequently been implemented in the same organization in a piecemeal or 'bolt-on' fashion. Performance management takes an holistic approach and integrates human resource and management systems with the aim of continuously improving organizational performance. Figure 2.5 shows the wide number of management techniques and initiatives which could potentially come under the umbrella of a performance management philosophy.

Target setting complements performance management and as can be seen from Figure 2.5 this may include targets which are set for individuals or working groups and which relate to individual or organizational objectives. Target setting offers the advantage of being able to define goals which relate to organizational aims at the same time as providing the flexibility of being able to tailor targets to the needs of individual employees.

Case Study – The Potential Pitfalls of Performance Appraisal

The Organization

Higgins and York are a well established professional partnership traditionally renowned for their quantity surveying expertise but recently they

The Context of Target Setting

have broadened into the field of estates management. They thrived in the period after World War II and their reputation was established largely as a result of the charisma and connections of the founding partners. In recent years they have found their market share eroded with the advent of a number of much younger, more commercial and dynamic organizations.

In response to this external pressure a recent merger has taken place with an historic competitor, due to the manoeuvring of some of the more progressive senior partners. Some of the 'old school' professionals see this as the inevitable but unwanted change which signals the decline of the industry as they knew it. In fact it marks the decline of the 'old boy network' as a way of doing business.

Senior level teams from the other organization were tasked with introducing some of their good human resource practices into Higgins and York. This included the introduction of a new performance appraisal scheme. Until now Higgins and York have viewed such techniques as 'soft' and not really relevant to their sector.

The People

Ernest is an experienced, professionally qualified manager who has been with Higgins and York all his career and feels concerned by a number of the changes taking place in the industry. He also feels threatened by the recent merger of the organizations. In his day, he maintains, it would have been unthinkable to merge. Recently a redundancy campaign was completed and Ernest had hoped to secure voluntary redundancy associated with preserved pension rights. He was turned down and has now reconciled himself to the fact that he will need to 'keep his head down' and see how things work out for the future.

A year ago a recent graduate, Tom, was transferred into Ernest's department. Tom was recruited a few years ago as part of an initiative to bring new blood into the organization. Tom is partly qualified, bright and hungry for success and progression. He sees the merger as a great opportunity to make a name for himself with what will become a major player in the market. Ernest accepted Tom into his department under some duress while having to acknowledge his strength and enthusiasm.

The Appraisal

Tom was told on Friday by Ernest's secretary that his appraisal would take place on Monday morning. He was given no information about what would be expected of him or how the appraisal meeting would be structured but was hopeful that it would provide an opportunity to agree the areas where he had been successful in recent months since joining the department and possibly he might obtain support from the organization to attend a day-release programme so that he could complete his professional studies. He was a little concerned about some reports he had heard from colleagues in the department about their appraisals. Some said they were not really given a fair chance to input to the discussion so Tom decided to prepare some thoughts on paper in anticipation of the meeting. Generally he felt he had been doing well, certainly feedback from clients and other senior managers had borne this out. Although he had taken this commonsense approach he did worry over the weekend about how the meeting would go, conscious of the fact that this was a watershed in his career.

He had received very little feedback from Ernest during the year regarding his progress, but then he did not feel unique in this respect. It was generally accepted in the department that Ernest, while well respected for his experience, was not too comfortable talking to staff about their performance or anything rather more personal than simply the technical aspects of the job. It was also known that Ernest had managed to avoid the performance appraisal training which the organization had recently arranged believing that there was not much they could teach him about management of people. It was also rumoured that he had had a less than easy time in his own appraisal with a number of his shortcomings being discussed for the first time in his career.

On Monday Tom had to see Ernest about a technical matter relating to a recent contract; the meeting was dragging on and Tom reminded Ernest about the booking he had for the appraisal meeting. Ernest said that they were too busy to cover it on the Monday and it could be 'knocked off' on the following day. Tom felt rather disappointed because, despite his worries, he had been anticipating the opportunity to discuss his performance with a hint of excitement.

On Tuesday the meeting lasted all of ten minutes! Tom was summoned to Ernest's office by his secretary and it was quite apparent that Ernest was nervous and keen to complete the meeting as soon as possible. He spent most of the time shuffling his papers and referring back to some guide notes. The conversation was very much one way and consisted of Ernest reading through a list of attributes Tom had never come across before and then reading out a grade. Grudgingly Tom was given a few good grades but was pulled up on a number of issues that he suspected were the same areas that Ernest himself had been criticized in. The main involvement that Tom had was to sign off the form at the end of the meeting: he did so but with reservations.

The Context of Target Setting

Outcome

On reflection Tom was sorely disappointed about his appraisal; he confided in some of his friends about it, one of whom studied at college with him and now worked for a competitor. This friend had mentioned some time ago that there was a vacancy in his organization and 'wouldn't it be good if they could work together'. Originally he had dismissed the idea, particularly when he heard of the Higgins and York merger as he thought he would channel all his energies into developing a successful career with them. His friend mentioned that there was still a vacancy and suggested that Tom should come along for an informal discussion. Initially Tom declined but eventually he was persuaded that there would be nothing to lose in just making contact.

At the informal interview he was most impressed with the professionalism of the people and the environment, and to his surprise he was offered a position with the opportunity to complete his professional qualification through a sponsored open learning programme. The salary offered was similar to that which he commanded at Higgins and York but the opportunities for development seemed much more attractive. He accepted the offer, gave in his notice with Higgins and York and left the organization just four weeks after his fateful performance appraisal interview.

> ### ACTIVITY
>
> Considering the case of Ernest and Tom at Higgins and York, list the various pitfalls which were encountered regarding performance appraisal. If you were responsible for the successful implementation of performance appraisal at Higgins and York what would you like to see handled differently? Suggested answers can be found in Appendix 1 on p109.

3 Integrating Target Setting with Existing Systems

▷   SUMMARY   ◁

In this chapter we emphasize the importance of integrating target setting with other organizational and human resource initiatives and systems. The number of such initiatives and systems is potentially great but particular coverage is given here to some of the most important and topical:
- reward and remuneration systems;
- competencies;
- training and development programmes;
- total quality management.

It is likely that trainers will have a role in designing or implementing such initiatives and they should take a holistic approach, constantly seeking integration and links rather than 'bolting' target setting on to existing systems.

We have seen how target setting sits comfortably within the context of performance appraisal. It is worth considering how a target setting initiative might fit with other organizational development initiatives which have emerged in recent years. The danger of attempting to implement target setting without considering how it relates to other human resource initiatives is that it will founder; the accusation from line management could be that it is 'just another scheme dreamt up by the personnel department' or that it involves 'more paperwork and administration; why can't we just get on with the job?'. For those responsible for introducing target setting the role can be made much easier by anticipating answers to questions such as 'But how does target setting fit in with total quality management/senior management training programme/competencies?' etc. Consideration of these issues demands strategic thinking on the part of the personnel or training specialist. We will consider some of the most relevant strategic issues below.

The Context of Target Setting

Reward and Remuneration Systems

A perennial debate in the field of performance appraisal is about whether the results of the appraisal interview should be linked to the reward system. In other words should a good performance appraisal interview mean a good pay review? Remuneration systems differ widely across organizations but with the growth of performance management and increasing competition it has become generally accepted that, while specific methods of remuneration may differ, the overall logic of rewarding good performance is likely to encourage good practice. Many organizations in the private sector and increasingly in the public sector have created an atmosphere of meritocracy. The corollary of this is that there should be some connection between the process of assessing performance, ie performance appraisal or the measurement of the achievement of targets, and the system for rewarding performance.

In principle this sounds very sensible, however there are a number of difficulties associated with this approach. First, if employees being assessed are aware that there will be a direct and immediate link to a salary review they are quite likely to attempt to seek maximum personal gain. In extreme cases this can mean a tactical approach on the part of an employee. Tactics could include overemphasizing successes and strengths, playing down weaknesses and approaching the review of targets as a negotiation rather than as a joint problem-solving discussion. This hardly creates the environment for the healthy two-way process referred to in the previous chapter.

To ignore the subject of rewards, however, can be equally destructive. There has been much debate and research into the motivational effects of pay and the summary of Charles Handy (1981) in his book *Understanding Organizations* makes some apposite comments. Firstly the tendency of money to motivate will vary for different individuals and it should be considered as potentially the means of satisfying a number of human needs. This will include, for example, physiological needs such as shelter or food, or status needs such as being able to purchase the latest model car or a larger house. Second, money tends to be used as the basis for comparison with others. Rewards are considered in relation to the rewards offered to those about whom the individual has a concept of his or her relative self-worth and this is likely to be a source of satisfaction or dissatisfaction. Relativity is often considered more important than the actual level of pay. Finally, a key motivator is often the fact that the individual has the ability to control the level of his or her income. This suggests that standard increments or across-the-board percentages are likely to be less motivational than, for example rewards related to the achievement of individual targets.

At the time he wrote them, Handy's comments on performance-related pay may have been correct: 'Only entrepreneurs and insurance salesmen, among executives, experience money tied to particular pieces of effort. They are known to be particularly motivated by money'. There has, however, been a great spread in the practice of rewarding performance through payment systems and it is quite normal now to find performance-related pay schemes in white-collar and blue-collar, professional, service, product, private and public-sector environments.

Given that it will not be uncommon for senior management, human resource or training specialists to introduce target setting in an organization where there is some form of performance-related pay, we should consider the practicalities of how to make appropriate connections between the achievement of targets and rewards. A key factor here is timing. If the pay award is to be made immediately after the review of performance against targets then clearly the review process will be emotionally charged and the risk of being drawn into the tactical game described previously will be high. If the review of targets is conducted some months before the salary review the emphasis can be placed more realistically on the subject of the targets themselves, how well they have been achieved, and the identification of targets for the future. Obviously when it comes to the actual salary review there will need to be some consideration of performance since the main target review to take into account any dramatic upturn or downturn in performance.

The other issue to consider is the extent to which the achievement of targets alone will affect the total remuneration package. Later in the book we emphasize that, while targets focus on key areas where successful performance will make an impact on the department and ultimately the organization, they do not necessarily cover the total job description. In other words it would be quite possible for an individual to fail to meet certain requirements of the job not identified in targets and for this to have a serious effect on the assessment of performance. For example timekeeping, manner in dealing with customers and attention to detail could be important qualities in a job: if standards are not maintained at a minimum level they could result in the tenability of the employees' position being brought into question. These qualities might not, however, form the basis of targets which would focus on overarching and forward looking subjects. When integrating a performance-related pay system and target setting it is important to consider which aspects of performance will have a direct impact on remuneration: what should be the balance in terms of targeted and non-targeted areas?

Similarly salary reviews which include an element of performance-related pay often include other components not necessarily related to individual performance such as a percentage linked to inflation, consideration of local market rates or industry-specific rates. Again it is important to distinguish clearly between these elements of the remuneration package and those linked to the achievements of targets.

It is worth noting that a recent study of performance management in the UK backed up previous research which failed to prove that there is a demonstrable link between performance-related payment systems and organizational performance (IPM, 1992). There is a danger then, in placing too much emphasis on remuneration at the expense of the 'softer' issues such as training and development.

Competencies

The 1980s saw the emergence in the UK of the 'competency movement' which has attempted to define the key areas of required performance in a job so that a recognized framework of competencies can be used for a number of applications in human resource management including, for example, recruitment and selection, training and development and succession planning. There have been many attempts to define what is actually meant by the term 'competence', the most appropriate and user friendly being 'The ability to apply knowledge and skill in the work situation and sustain performance over a period of time'. A key point here is the emphasis on the application of knowledge and skills. As training and education provision has evolved there has been a tendency for the development of knowledge and skills to take place in the off-job situation such as the classroom or management training centre with the inherent difficulties of transfer of learning to the workplace. The competency approach links the areas of skill and knowledge development to application, leaving open the way in which development might take place.

In the UK this thinking has led to the development of qualifications that can be achieved in the workplace. These National Vocational Qualifications are achieved by working to standards which are expressed in the form of competencies. Such competencies have been defined on either an industry basis (for example engineering, hairdressing, retail) or to cover occupations which cross industrial sectors (such as clerical skills and management). The intention has been to define generic competencies which are applicable in all organizations operating in the given industry or to all occupations in the relevant field. This has been a controversial exercise but there is no doubt that it has led to a quantum leap in our understanding of how the competency approach can be applied in practice. Figure 3.1 shows the key roles and their associated units of competency for the middle management role as defined by the industry lead body for management, the Management Charter Initiative (1991).

Key Role	Units
Manage operations	1 Maintain and improve service and product operations.
	2 Contribute to the implementation of change in services, products and systems.
Manage finance	3 Recommend, monitor and control the use of resources.
Manage people	4 Contribute to the recruitment and selection of personnel.
	5 Develop teams, individuals and self to enhance performance.
	6 Plan, allocate and evaluate work carried out by teams, individuals and self.
	7 Create, maintain and enhance effective working relationships.
Manage information	8 Seek, evaluate and organize information for action.
	9 Exchange information to solve problems and make decisions.

Figure 3.1 *Key roles of management and their associated units of competence (Crown copyright)*

Some organizations have been quicker to draw on such work in the competency field than others. Unfortunately some have interpreted the publication of such competency lists as implying a straitjacket which does not fit well with the peculiarities of their own organization. Some, however, have realized that such systems need not be followed slavishly nor should they exclude the organization from enhancing the competency list with additional or supplementary competencies which are more relevant for them.

Having defined the required areas of competency for different roles in an organization the framework of competencies can be used in a number of ways to provide the 'cement' which binds and strengthens many human resource initiatives. For instance, competencies can form the basis for selection criteria against specific positions. They can be highlighted in job descriptions, person specifications, interview plans and

The Context of Target Setting

might form the basis of criteria used in selection testing. Equally they can define subject areas for training and development programmes and might form a useful reference point in discussing individual training and development needs. Competencies can also help to define the subject of individual targets. Logically, if competencies attempt to define the requirements for effective job performance and targets are supposed to give individuals clear objectives for self development and organizational impact, then the two subjects cannot possibly be considered in isolation in the same organization. Figure 3.2 identifies some of the connections between competencies designed for the industry or organization and the types of target which might be considered appropriate in order to help employees develop competence.

Organizational Comptencies	**Individual Targets**
Generic competencies – defined by industry or function	Technical/skill-based targets, eg team building, financial techniques.
Departmental/sectional competencies	Locally applicable targets, eg use of a particular computing system, building relationships with other departments.
Personal competencies	Personal development targets, eg interpersonal skills, self-management skills.

Figure 3.2 Linking individual targets to organizational competencies

For target setting to be of value for individuals it is necessary to ensure that targets do not simply replicate the competency framework, but use it to help provide a basis for identifying targets which are of relevance to the employee.

Training and Development Programmes

Many organizations are introducing major culture change programmes in order to improve their competitive edge and survive in a dynamic business environment. Usually a major vehicle for such programmes is a series of training and development workshops or courses. Individual target setting can reinforce the messages behind culture change programmes by building core themes into targets. For example if one of the key culture change themes is to increase proactivity then an individual target might focus on ways in which the employee could operate in a more proactive fashion at a local level. In this specific case the target could include, for example, subjects such as building external contacts, initiating new projects, or exercising more creativity.

Another major development in the field of training has been the tendency to coordinate different employee development interventions such as off-job courses, on-job development and educational training. The concept of the 'learning organization' suggests that the organization should constantly transform itself by learning from everything it does and that in the future this is how competitive edge will be gained: through the ability and willingness of employees to learn constantly. In a sense there are mixed messages here. On the one hand any learning is good learning because it helps people learn to learn which is an increasingly important skill in its own right. On the other hand the provision of training in successful organizations is becoming better coordinated, themed and linked to strategic plans.

With either scenario target setting can provide a vital link between the identification of individual training needs and support for corporate training programmes. In the more forward thinking organizations training needs are identified in order to help employees achieve future targets as opposed to providing remedial training for those whose weaknesses are exposed after being promoted to their level of incompetence: the 'push' rather than 'pull' approach.

Total Quality Management

Due in major part to the pioneering work of an American statistician, Dr W Edwards Deming, Japanese industry, which in the postwar period was notorious for producing poor quality products, became a major force in world markets. The turnaround was remarkable and the key was quality. Ironically Deming had previously failed to convince his compatriots that focusing on quality was so important and only by questioning and learning from the success of the Japanese did total quality management (TQM) concepts take root in the Western world. It is now difficult to find a sector which has not been touched by the quality revolution as organizations strive to meet the increasing expectations of customers, manage their supply chain more comfortably and differentiate themselves from the competition.

Total quality initatives can utilize different techniques and may have a subtly different emphasis when implemented across organizations, but there are common underpinning principles. Some of the key messages behind TQM are listed in Figure 3.3.

- Continuously satisfying the needs of the customer
- Redefinition of customer to include internal customers
- Getting it right first time, every time, on time
- Quality thinking runs throughout the whole organization and applies to all levels and functions
- Closer relationships with customers and suppliers
- Delegation of decision making and problem solving to the lowest level of the organizational structure
- Valuing the potential of all staff regardless of status
- Never walking past poor quality – everyone has a responsibility for quality
- Measurement of performance and establishing standards and targets
- Continuous improvement – the *kaisen* concept in Japan
- High-profile training to implement total quality management which is followed through

Figure 3.3 *Total quality management principles*

TQM is essentially a philosophy rather than a technique and as such serves to facilitate consistent quality thinking throughout the whole organization at all levels and across all functions. In order to achieve this focusing of all employees in the same direction a range of effective techniques has evolved. Two of the key techniques which relate most obviously to target setting are developments in the field of problem solving and decision making and the concept of quality circles. We will consider these in turn and look at how target setting can contribute to their successful implementation.

Problem Solving and Decision Making

It has long been considered that one of the primary roles of management is to oversee the succesful completion of tasks and to use financial and human resources to achieve this. Implied in this approach is the fact that the responsibility for defining problems and making decisions regarding their solution lies with management. Taking this approach to the extreme the autocratic style of management works on the basis that managers tell 'workers' what to do, reward those who do it and discipline those who do not. This is a crude summary but highlights the contrast with the more successful and democratic approach espoused by TQM organizations which value the contribution that all employees have to make. The TQM approach recognizes that by helping all employees to identify organizational or operational problems and by equipping them with the skills to work towards their solution, the task of management is redefined. Rather than managers continually having to 'fire-fight' and being forced to operate in a reactive mode because they assume total responsibility for solving all problems they are able to devolve some of this burden to others. Furthermore there are likely to be less fires to fight under TQM because problems are proactively sought out and anticipated rather than simply reacted to. The priorities for managers in TQM organizations are to coach and encourage staff so that they develop problem-solving and decision-making abilities.

One of the major causes of failure of TQM implementation is that an initiative is launched with much enthusiasm and hype but initial training is not followed through with those who have to make it work. Problem-solving and decision-making skills develop over time with practice and employees need help in knowing when to apply specific approaches. This does not come simply with an initial training course; there is a need to provide continual follow-up support and this support becomes particularly powerful if it is built into individual targets. For example, at the target setting stage it might be possible to agree targets which reinforce TQM concepts by focusing on the following areas:

- developing problem-solving skills through off-job training;
- demonstrating problem-solving ability by identifying key areas to focus on and coordinating quality circles in working towards suggested solutions;
- demonstrating the successful application of problem-solving techniques eg brainstorming, mind mapping, cost–benefit analysis, fishbone diagrams, force-field analysis;
- reducing the number of problems requiring crisis action through a proactive approach to anticipating problems.

Clearly these examples do not constitute targets per se, but could well form the basis for targets which would be agreed in detail following the guidance provided in Chapter 5.

The Context of Target Setting

Quality Circles

Those organizations which have introduced the quality circle concept most successfully have done so by translating the Japanese concept of work improvement groups into a language and style most appropriate to their existing culture rather than relying on direct mimicry. They have also integrated the quality circle approach into the wider context of TQM rather than relying on quality circles as a stand-alone initiative. In essence the quality circle approach is simple: small groups, typically comprising seven to ten employees, based on voluntary membership, come together to solve work-based problems which they themselves identify. This approach accepts that those actually doing the job are best placed to identify problems and propose solutions. Quality circles might comprise those at the lower end of the organization structure in shaping work methods and priorities.

As with TQM in general one of the potential pitfalls with quality circles is that following the enthusiasm generated by the initial training programme there is little follow-up support for employees: the principle of delegation in fact results in abdication and there are no support structures to equip or encourage quality circle members to succeed.

As with problem solving and decision making, target setting provides the opportunity to give management support to quality circle members; quality circle concepts can be integrated into the everyday job. Subjects for individual targets could include:

- teambuilding;
- working in groups;
- presenting ideas to senior management;
- influencing upwards in the organization;
- meetings skills; and
- handling conflict.

Such skills, which are necessary for employees to be able to make a successful contribution to quality circles, are not developed by one-off training courses alone; it is essential to provide continual development opportunities and the facility to practise relevant skills and build confidence over time. Well defined targets can help to ensure that quality circles do not collapse due to lack of support beyond the initial stage of formation.

Target setting might potentially impact upon a very large number of organizational or human resource initatives and policies. We have considered some of the most important and topical ones, but it is vital for those responsible for the implementation of target setting, especially the professional trainer, consciously to work through the connections with those initiatives and policies operational in their own organization. Consideration will need to be given to the history and culture of the organization. In particular, when introducing target setting it is important to know whether management by objectives or performance appraisal schemes have been introduced before and how successfully. Anticipating these issues will help to determine which matters to emphasize when implementing target setting and delivering associated training. Success is more likely when there is an integrated approach to human resource management and activities are related to the needs of the organization. It is equally important both to focus on targets linked to developmental initiatives such as training and development and culture change and to make connections with the 'harder' issues such as remuneration and payment systems.

ACTIVITY

Consider the human resource management and organizational initiatives which have been introduced in your organization:
- When were they introduced and how successfully?
- Which initiatives can be directly linked to target setting?
- Which initiatives are less directly linked to target setting?
- Try to anticipate the questions which might be raised by employees at different levels and in different functions of your organization about the connection between target setting and existing initiatives.

4 Preparing the Organization for Success through Target Setting

> ▷ SUMMARY ◁
>
> In this chapter we consider some of the problems associated with establishing targets in specific types of job function or role. By anticipating these issues it is likely that the human resource specialist or trainer responsible for implementing target setting will be in a stronger position to deal with the reservations that will be encountered in different sectors of the organization. Specifically we will consider target setting for:
>
> - those under time pressure;
> - senior managers;
> - administrative or service function staff;
> - technical staff;
> - valued employees who do not wish to progress through the organizational hierarchy; and
> - those who may be ambitious but realistically are not going to progress further internally.
>
> By anticipating the difficulties of implementing target setting in their own organization, trainers will be equipped to take a proactive approach to dealing with the various concerns of employees.

The success of any target setting initiative is dependent largely on how it is implemented; it is quite possible to have an elegantly designed system that fails due to problems associated with implementation. We will look in detail at the subject of training managers and employees in the skills of target setting and review in Part III but it is also worth anticipating the many objections to target setting which occur as it is introduced in different functions and at all levels of the organization.

Often the individual will give various reasons as to why it is not practicable to set targets in their own job role or discipline. Sometimes there is simply lack of ability to see how targets can actually be set for a particular function: often the root cause of this concern is the fact that the individual automatically associates targets with quantitative measures such as sales made, units produced, labour turnover or profit. Additionally there is frequently an underlying fear that working to targets will mean that supervision will be tightened, discretion for the individual decreased and that the employee's every move will be scrutinized.

It is also usual for employees to see targets as linked to personal development and, by association, with career development and progression. For some this will be seen as an opportunity to gain recognition for their achievements; for others, however, it may be viewed as a threat or pressure, particularly for those who are less ambitious or lack confidence in their own ability to progress. One of the most common reasons initially given for not being able to set targets is lack of time: target setting is seen as another burden to be imposed on the already busy manager.

By anticipating these objections and working through ways of recognizing and dealing with them the implementation of a target setting initiative is more likely to succeed.

Time Constraints

One common problem in implementing any human resource policy is that of encouraging managers to take ownership for what are considered to be initiatives which are in the best interest of the organization. The role of the human resource specialist, and in particular the trainer, has shifted from that of imposing and policing organizational change to one of facilitating change and enabling managers to develop 'best practice'. In organizations where the history of the human resource function has fitted with the old style, the introduction of target setting can easily be interpreted as 'just another scheme from personnel'. The predisposition of managers is likely to be dismissive and less likely to be cooperative where they feel that their time would be better spent pursuing activities relevant to their line function. This is much more likely to be the case where human resource systems carry with them excessive documentation and involve the completion of complex or extensive paperwork. The cry is bound to be 'Why don't they just leave me to get on with my job?'

An important point for trainers to consider when anticipating this argument is that for the manager under pressure through sheer workload and time constraints, target setting can actually help improve the ability to manage time and relieve stress. For managers who are stressed as a result of under-delegation and have a tendency to take on too much work, target setting provides a powerful lever for developing managerial styles that encourage the development of knowledge and skills among subordinates rather than feeling under pressure to hold personally all the expertise needed in the section or department. So for the trainer introducing target setting the sorts of question which should be considered in anticipation of objections due to lack of time include:

- What are you currently doing which you could hand over to your staff by setting effective targets?
- What knowledge do you hold which could usefully be shared with your staff or could be developed by your staff with guidance through target setting?
- What skills do you hold which, if developed by your staff, will relieve you of pressure? (For example chairing meetings, negotiating with suppliers and customers, controlling budgets or expenditure, recruitment, supervision of junior staff, report writing.)
- How could you coach your staff to take on some of your responsibilities?
- If you were being considered for promotion would a member of your staff be able to replace you? If not you may be restricting your chances of promotion!

The potential benefits of working through these questions are twofold. First, there is the opportunity to develop the skills of subordinates through effective target setting and then there is the opportunity to use this as a means of developing managers' skills in prioritization, delegation and developing people. Boyatsis (1982) found that skill in goal setting and planning was among the key determinants of a manager's success.

Furthermore, if there are targets being set at a managerial level and there are objections on the basis of time this may point to the need for the development of time-management skills. This need too can be reinforced through a target setting initiative. So the manager might work towards targets such as:

Develop time management skills over the next six months so that you

are able to allocate around 25 per cent of work time to developmental, future focused activity. To facilitate this you will
1 attend a short off-job time management training programme and implement time management techniques which have been learned;
2 share knowledge and skills with staff through an ongoing coaching initiative which will enable delegation of certain responsibilities.

Success will be measured by studying the amount of developmental compared with operational work being conducted in the working week without the need to work over and above normal working hours; to be reviewed at the end of a six-month period.

Seniority

One of the most difficult areas to establish targets of a behavioural or developmental nature is among senior management. The natural tendency is to suggest that targets at a senior level should only relate to easily measured factors such as sales, profit or production. Indeed it may well be appropriate to measure success in these terms but it can be hazardous to place all the emphasis on such results at the expense of some of the target areas which have traditionally been considered less measurable and 'softer'. For example it could be quite appropriate for a production manager to work towards a production target – say 3000 units per month, but if in achieving this target he or she manages to destroy relationships with suppliers, exhaust the production team and damage the reputation of the production department within the organization then the original target might have been better unachieved. While short-term and easily measured production targets might be met, long term the likelihood of continuing to meet them is greatly reduced. What is equally damaging is the fact that the production manager may have reduced the likelihood of a number of other people achieving their own targets.

Another major problem experienced by managers moving into senior level positions is a natural tendency to revert to carrying out the functions of their old job which they understand better and feel more comfortable with. Ultimately this will frustrate staff below who had seen their own promotion as an opportunity to develop new skills and experience but who too are pushed back into carrying out their old job. This is expressed well by Bob Garatt (1990) in his book *Creating a Learning Organization* and the key message is that we actually neglect managers once they reach the most senior positions in the organization in terms of training and development. The difficulty is often knowing what sort of training is really appropriate for general management and the natural inclination is simply to provide coverage of the same functional topics as those provided at lower levels of the organization but to dress them up as 'senior management programmes'. As there may be no formal training for the most senior managers it is often assumed that they have demonstrated sufficient potential to deserve their exalted positions and therefore do not need further training: all too often it is a case of 'sink or swim'.

Targets provide a unique opportunity to tackle this issue head on, without publicly making the newly appointed senior manager feel even more vulnerable and isolated. Targets could be agreed to cover such issues as:

- understanding the finance of the organization;
- understanding the market place/industry;
- the nature of the competition;
- learning about other functions;
- relating external trends and influences to the organization;
- developing the profile of the organization;
- strategic decision making;
- developing managers;
- improving internal communications;
- special technical projects; or
- organizational change.

Involving senior managers in the implementation of a target setting initiative is a vital ingredient for success. As soon as employees detect that there is not genuine commitment from the top the whole programme becomes devalued and will slide down the priority list for busy managers. A very powerful strategy is to involve senior management in the launch of the target setting initiative by, for example, asking them to publicize target setting and to support it overtly. Taking this one step further it is extremely effective if senior managers are involved in the actual implementation of the programme through, for example:

- inputting to parts of the training programme;
- running training workshops unaided;
- demonstrating that they are working to targets themselves; or
- requesting that targets are reported upwards once set.

Involving senior managers in running training workshops or in appearing for guest slots can prove to be a subtle means of developing the target setting skills and awareness of the senior managers without exposing them as delegates on training courses where they might feel inhibited through a sense of vulnerability. Every time managers contribute to a training workshop they will be buying into the process at the same time as making a clear statement to employees that senior management is committed to target setting.

Administrative and Service Functions

Frequently staff in administrative or service functions will feel that it is inappropriate if not impossible to set targets in their particular area of the business. Often this is due largely to the tendency to associate targets with functions having an obvious link with the success of business such as sales or production. Also for those in a support or staff function it may be felt that it is difficult to measure performance. Employees in a job role where they have little discretion over what they do, and where workload and the type of work is determined by outside forces, may feel that it is unfair to expect that targets can realistically be established. For example for a cashier in a bank it might be considered that to set a target for generating leads for new business from contact with existing customers is unfair. This is because the cashier has no control over the number of customers using the bank. The number of customers could be influenced by factors such as the economy, the competition and the effectiveness of the sales and marketing department. Similarly managers should be cautious in selecting subjects for targets which actually relate to standards which ought to be maintained as a normal part of the employee's job function. It is important to balance these standards-related criteria with targets that will help the individual and the organization move successfully into the future. Listed below are some examples of the sorts of subject which relate more to the maintenance of standards than individual development targets in service or administrative roles:

1 Maintain a level of absence through sickness of no more than five days per year.
2 Ensure work benches and machines are cleaned and tidied at the end of each day by commencing the clearing up procedure no sooner than ten minutes before the end of the shift.
3 Adhere to health and safety procedures and reduce the number of accidents in the workplace.
4 Maintain spending levels within the annual budget figures as agreed at the start of the financial year.
5 Halve the number of customer complaints over the next six-month period.

6 Respond to job applications within one week of receiving letters from applicants.

While each of these may be appropriate standards for different job roles they do not constitute developmental targets as such; they are standards which should be maintained and there is really no acceptable standard beyond:

1 No absence through sickness.
2 Total cleanliness of work areas.
3 No accidents.
4 No overspend.
5 No customer complaints.
6 No delay on response to applicants.

A number of organizations are successfully bringing about major quality improvements by focusing on such specific measures, identifying current performance and establishing improvements required. These measures are appropriate for groups of employees to work towards and by focusing on the achievement of incremental gains it is possible to contribute to the creation of a continuous improvement culture which can have major cost-saving effects for the organization. Such subjects, should, however, be balanced with targets which have a more personal value for individuals who work towards them in terms of their own development.

While some targets of this nature might be appropriate for groups of employees where they carry out similar roles, it is just as possible to design targets which have a high personal value for those in service or administrative positions. Some organizations with groups of employees who carry out the same job role successfully identify some common objectives and then use individually tailored targets to help individuals develop depending on their own personal needs. This is a realistic way of acknowledging that generally similar job roles are being carried out and in many areas consistent standards are expected, but that each employee is unique and the organization recognizes they will have their own individual development needs. Some examples of individual targets for employees in administrative and service roles are shown in Figure 4.1 It can be seen in these two examples that the target specified serves two purposes:

1 It offers a means for the individual to perform more effectively and demonstrates that the organization is prepared to make resources available for this development.
2 It will clearly help the department and ultimately the organization in terms of two key service functions being carried out more effectively in the future.

Job Role	Example of Target
Personnel Assistant	Develop and maintain effective use of the computerized personnel records system. Accurate records of employee details when checked against manually held information and production of error-free monthly reports. Successful retrieval of user friendly information for line management, demonstrated by good feedback from managers. Initial training on the system to be provided by short off-job training course given by the software supplier and then by ongoing coaching from the internal technical support department over the next six months. Progress to be monitored on an ongoing basis and reviewed after six months.
Receptionist	To develop an understanding of the structure of the organization's functions and different departments. To be able to recognize key managers at section level and above and to be able to recall the function of their department. This is to help familiarize the receptionist with the organization and the industry and will help when processing enquiries from visitors and callers. Progress to be monitored regularly and reviewed after three months. Methods will include obtaining literature relating to the structure and nature of the business, inclusion on circulation lists regarding personnel changes. It is expected that after three months the job holder would be able to escort a visitor or a new joiner on a tour of the offices, providing an introductory explanation of the functions of each section.

Figure 4.1 *Examples of targets in administrative or service roles*

The Context of Target Setting

Increasingly organizations are recognizing that there are internal customer/supplier relationships and that the key is to identify these links and focus effort on improving the service that a department or individual provides to the internal customer. This will ultimately lead to increased competitiveness externally. Quality consultants have estimated (DTI, 1991) that savings of up to 25 per cent of turnover can be made through this focus on quality service. For the personnel assistant's job role identified in Figure 4.1 the possible customer/supplier relationships are shown in Figure 4.2. In target setting for the whole job it would be appropriate to define similar targets which focus on the needs of all categories of customer.

Suppliers	Jobholder	Customers
EXTERNAL SOFTWARE SUPPLIER		CUSTOMER 1 Line managers assessing personnel records to help in monitoring human resource status in their departments.
INTERNAL TECHNICAL SUPPORT DEPARTMENT	PERSONNEL ASSISTANT	CUSTOMER 2 Personnel department using the personnel records for strategic decision making.
		CUSTOMER 3 External organizations requiring information on human resource utilization for equal opportunities monitoring, data protection and local employment statistical purposes.

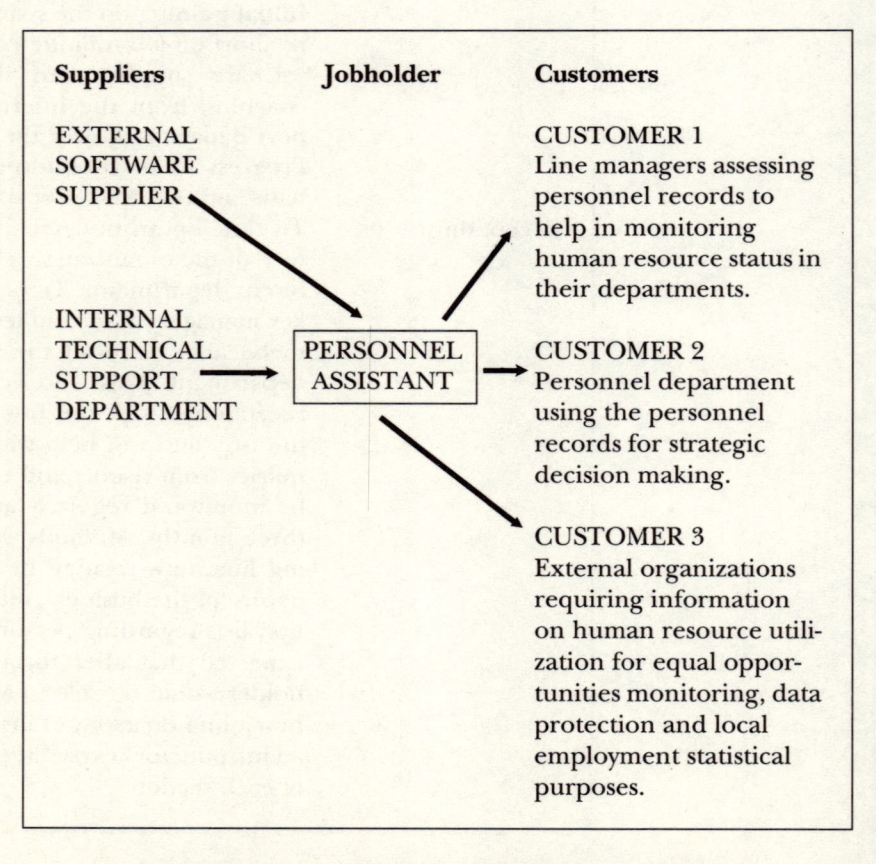

Figure 4.2 *Customer/supplier relationships for the role of personnel assistant*

To help you understand the importance of service departments setting targets which relate to improved service to their customers you might like to attempt the following exercise:

> **DEFINING TARGETS FOR SERVICE FUNCTIONS**
>
> Figure 4.1 provides a detailed target for the personnel assistant regarding the relationship with Customers 1 and 2 as shown in Figure 4.2, that is line management and the personnel department. Using this as a model target, now attempt to devise targets as follows:
>
> 1. For the personnel assistant servicing Customer 3 – external organizations seeking information for equal opportunities monitoring, data protection and local employment statistical reporting purposes.
> 2. For the external software supplier providing a service, ie design, provision and maintenance of a software system for the personnel assistant.
> 3. For the internal technical support department providing a service to the personnel assistant to help develop understanding of the system and deal with technical problems.
> 4. Now you might like to identify the internal and external customer/supplier relationships for the receptionist identified in Figure 4.1 and design targets for the various suppliers in the relationship as you have done for the personnel assistant.

Targets for Technical Roles

In technical organizations or departments it is common to face objections to target setting on the grounds that 'It is impossible to set targets here because we are too technical'. True it may be difficult to set targets due to the technical nature of a job and it may be problematic for the human resource specialist or trainer who may not have a technical background to understand all the details of specific job functions. This, however, is no reason for exempting technical departments from an organization-wide target setting initiative.

The Context of Target Setting

The key advice for those responsible for putting target setting into place in this sort of department is to work on two types of target: the technical target and the behavioural or developmental target. It may be quite possible to set technical targets which need to be agreed by a line manager who has an understanding of such issues and would be able to assess what would constitute a realistic, achievable and stretching technical target. Some examples of targets which have been set in technical organizations or departments are given in Figure 4.3.

Job Role	Example of a Technical Target
Network manager	Update and improve the network help desk operations procedures over the next six months focusing on the following: • Attend helpdesk management training course and use skills developed to guide network operations staff. • Produce a helpdesk user document which will be publicised and enable users to follow appropriate procedures. Success to be reviewed through feedback from users and review of the user document after a six-month period.
Engineering supervisor	Train shopfloor staff in the use of the new cutting machine so that they are able to set up, operate and carry out routine maintenance knowing when to draw on external help. Ensure staff are able to clean and close down machines without assistance within the next two months. This will be achieved by developing a written training programme and instruction manual.
Maintenance technician	Implement design modifications to the ZY product instrumentation which will satisfy the requirements of the test department within the next month. Design costs should remain within the budgetary constraints as agreed. Assistance where needed to be provided by the engineering

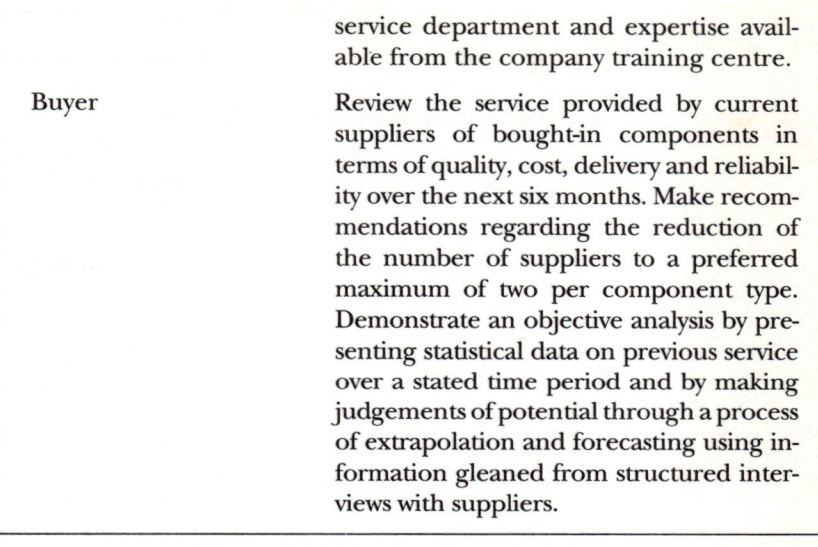

	service department and expertise available from the company training centre.
Buyer	Review the service provided by current suppliers of bought-in components in terms of quality, cost, delivery and reliability over the next six months. Make recommendations regarding the reduction of the number of suppliers to a preferred maximum of two per component type. Demonstrate an objective analysis by presenting statistical data on previous service over a stated time period and by making judgements of potential through a process of extrapolation and forecasting using information gleaned from structured interviews with suppliers.

Figure 4.3 *Examples of technical targets*

These examples may help in considering the types of technical target which are appropriate to your organization. In dealing with technical departments, having persuaded managers of the benefits and feasibility of setting technical targets, it is important to stress the significance of not being over reliant on technical subjects for target content. It is equally possible to identify behavioural and developmental targets which can make an important impact on the department: it is natural however that technical managers will initially focus on the technicalities of the job role.

In terms of personal development some subjects for non-technical targets which could be introduced to technical departments are shown in Figure 4.4.

It can be seen that developmental targets might focus on issues such as the broadening of job roles and the development of interpersonal skills and supervisory management ability. For any employee in a technical role it is worth considering how specific technical skills can be balanced with such developmental objectives. Naturally the tendency of the technical experts will be to associate targets with the more technical achievements than the behavioural type of target. The role of the human resource specialist or trainer will be to broaden the technologist's concept of what constitutes a legitimate target.

Interestingly, similar barriers to target setting will be encountered in creative environments where employees are likely to believe that it is not possible to establish targets where they work on 'inspiration' which is

The Context of Target Setting

Job Role	Example of developmental target
Production operative	Develop awareness of production techniques outside of current area of work so that you are able to explain to other employees the flow of production from kitting, through assembly to final testing. This will also help in preparation for movement on to other sections of the production department and will develop multi-skilled expertise. This will be achieved by temporary placement in other sections when workflow allows and by studying work instruction manuals from other sections. Time period for being able to supervise new staff to the department is three months.
Hardware engineer	Develop interpersonal skills with particular emphasis on presentation and influence in meetings. This will be achieved by attending the company presentations skills training course and structured reading combined with a gradual increase in involvement in team meetings and ongoing review of development through discussions with the engineering manager. Success will be measured by the ability to chair departmental meetings in the absence of the engineering manager and on a presentation on the work of the department to be given to other departments by the end of a nine-month period.
Project supervisor	Develop skills of supervision by delegating responsibility and coaching in technical aspects of project administration. This will be aided by the completion of a supervisory education programme combining open learning with development days over the coming year. Success will be measured by reviewing the improve-

> ment in skills of staff and their ability to cope in their jobs without close day-to-day supervision. Measures of the current ability of staff will be agreed now and targets for individual development established. The departmental manager will offer support by way of regular discussion with the project supervisor.

Figure 4.4 *Examples of developmenetal targets for technical roles*

considered to be a natural phenomenon that might be stifled by the setting of targets. It is equally appropriate to focus on the developmental and behavioural types of target which have been shown in the context of technical roles. It is also possible to establish targets which in fact relate to the success of creative ideas.

Not Everyone wants to be Promoted – Not Everyone will be Promoted

A common and legitimate cry against establishing targets in certain parts of the organization is that not all employees are ambitious and hungry for progression up through the corporate ranks. This point is worthy of specific consideration because it is true that the normal reaction to performance appraisal and target setting is that it is all geared to preparing employees for career progression. Clearly not all employees are aiming to progress in terms of working their way through the hierarchy and may feel that promotion is either unrealistic or undesirable. This is not to suggest that such employees are to be in any way undervalued; often they form the lifeblood of the organization and with appropriate recognition will provide stability and continuity over a number of years.

It would be a mistake, however, to exclude such employees from the organization's target setting initiative; indeed establishing targets and reviewing them provides an opportunity to recognize the achievements of those who often feel ignored in the event of organizational development and progress. With major changes affecting all sectors of business and the need to improve continuously it is possible to help employees to cope with changing practices and develop new skills by agreeing targets which could focus on, for example, new knowledge required and new skills to be developed. Very few jobs will remain exactly the same in terms of content over a long period of time and it is possible to broaden the experience of employees without necessarily expecting them to progress

The Context of Target Setting

upwards. Including such employees in the target setting process may unleash unexpected potential, and the positive reinforcement which follows review of successfully achieved targets can maintain staff motivation at a higher level.

It is also important to recognize that some employees may reach a position where they are unable to progress upwards in the organization structure, yet are providing a valued contribution and, if suitably motivated, could continue to do so for some time. Often managers feel uncomfortable about developing such employees for fear of losing them to competitors. A broadminded approach to setting stretching targets in the current job role while recognizing that internal career progression opportunities are limited can in fact result in a useful contribution being made prior to an external career move, and is more likely to allow the employee to leave the organization on a high note.

ACTIVITY

Consider the various functions in your organization and attempt to anticipate the objections and barriers which will arise in response to a target setting initiative.

Against these objections and barriers attempt to outline some examples of targets which will prove to the doubters that target setting is not only possible but relevant and worthwhile. You may wish to refer back to some of the examples of targets given in this chapter to help trigger ideas.

II

The Practice of Target Setting

5 Target Setting in Practice

> ▷ **SUMMARY** ◁
>
> In this chapter we look at the practicalities of target setting. The following ground rules for effective target setting are established:
> - focus on expected outputs;
> - ensure a balance between quantitative and developmental targets;
> - invest time in agreeing success criteria – it pays off at assessment;
> - pitch targets so they are achievable but stretching;
> - demonstrate management support for the process through action;
> - involve employees in deciding their own target areas;
> - use targets to help manage change and establish organizational culture.

Having tracked the trends towards target setting and the importance of 'selling' the whole concept into the organization we now need to look at the practicalities of how to set targets for individual employees. As previously stated there is no job or department where it is impossible to set targets, but the target setting process raises particular problems for different functions and job roles. The trainer is a key player in ensuring that the good practices explained in this chapter are developed and spread throughout the organization.

It may help if you consider how you might apply the guidance given in this chapter to setting targets in your own job. Despite the particular problems of setting targets in different functions, eg sales, finance, production and personnel, there are a number of ground rules which will help when setting targets and ultimately will ensure that individuals contribute effectively to the success of the organization.

What are Targets?

Targets are often known by other names such as objectives and goals but really these terms all describe the same thing. Targets explain what should be achieved at the end of an activity – a point to be hit or a desired result. The emphasis in this definition is important because the focus is on output rather than input or effort. Of course a particular target may be very demanding in terms of effort required to achieve it but the emphasis in the output statement is on the fact that it is achieved rather than how it was achieved. The guidance on how to achieve the target is discussed and agreed once the target has been described in terms of an output statement.

Figure 5.1 gives examples of output statements compared with input statements. These output statements alone are not comprehensive targets but would form part of a series of sentences which would make up a target. It is, however, important to understand the key principle of output statements first.

Job Role	Input Statements	Output Statements
Secretarial	Double the amount of time spent on filing.	Ensure all documents are correctly filed within 24 hours of receipt.
Sales	Conduct a minimum of four sales visits per day to customers over the next six months.	Increase sales of product X by 20 per cent over the next six months and increase market share by 2 per cent.

Figure 5.1 *Input and output statements*

With the example shown of the secretarial input statement, doubling the amount of time spent on filing does not state the standard to be achieved or what level of efficiency is to be expected. The output statement, however, establishes a means of checking whether or not a target is actually achieved.

In the example of the sales input statement it would be possible to hit the target number of sales visits through increased effort but the effectiveness of such visits is not specified. With the sales output statement it might be possible by 'working smarter' rather than 'working harder' to achieve the sales target with fewer customer visits.

One of the first ground rules in target setting, then, is to include output statements. This does not mean simply attaching a figure to the target; we need to strike a conscious balance between what can be termed 'quantitative' and 'developmental' targets. Also it is equally important when setting quantitative targets to provide guidance on how they will be achieved.

Quantitative Targets

Take some time to consider examples of targets for job roles in your own organization. It is quite likely you initially thought of numerical targets such as:

- improve sales by 20 per cent;
- decrease errors by 70 per cent;
- achieve an efficiency ratio of 95 per cent on production machines;
- halve the number of customer complaints;
- produce 3000 units in the next month;
- recruit 30 graduate trainees by September;
- reduce the level of unauthorized absence to no more than six days per person in the rolling year;
- bring down labour turnover to under 6 per cent.

When realistically set these numerical targets are useful and they could apply at various levels: organizational, departmental or individual. If set for one person this type of target is geared towards the individual contributing to the wider aims of the business. Certainly if it is possible to build a realistic figure into such a target this will help both manager and subordinate share the same understanding of what is to be achieved. This will make assessment much easier at a later stage and ensure that there are no awkward discussions about what was originally agreed in terms of the degree of difficulty or standards. There are, however, dangers in relying too heavily on purely quantitative targets.

First, it is important when expressing a target in quantitative terms to provide some guidance on how the individual might achieve the numerical aspect of the target. If the figure relates to a departmental or organizational goal the target should be broken down to provide more specific guidance as in Figure 5.2. Here the detailed guidance is given on how the cost savings should be achieved. This will help provide focus for the employee and some concrete issues to concentrate on.

Function	Overall Numerical Target	More Detailed Guidance
Marketing	To save the department over £200,000 over the next financial year	Focus on effective buying of print materials and art work and negotiate discounts with quality external suppliers as well as making effective use of the internal print department.

Figure 5.2 *Building on numerical targets*

Second, when setting targets for a member of staff it is vital to strike a balance between targets which focus on the departmental or organizational goals and targets which are specifically intended to develop the individual. Obviously achieving the cost-saving target for the marketing department in the example may well involve the development of personal skills such as negotiation, costing and budgeting, but the primary focus is on the achievement of the departmental objective, ie saving £200,000.

Developmental Targets

Developmental targets on the other hand place the primary focus on developing the individual; they might relate to:

- learning a new skill;
- taking on more responsibility;
- improving a particular aspect of the individual's performance;
- increasing knowledge;
- developing interpersonal skills, etc.

The easiest way of checking whether a target is really a developmental target is to ask whether the person will take the view that 'there is something in achieving this target for me'. The individual must have a vested interest in achieving the target; it will give something of personal value. You might like to consider the developmental targets in Figure 5.3 and think of a target for your own job which you would see as developmental.

Type	Target	How to Achieve	Success Criteria
Supervisory	Take supervisory responsibility for the two clerical staff in the department.	Coaching and guidance from departmental manager over next three months. Attendance on off-job supervisory training course.	Minimal amount of day-to-day supervision needed. No major problems needing managerial intervention.
Technical	Develop spreadsheet skills.	Attend relevant training course. To be allocated reports which demand the setting up of spreadsheets.	Able to set up spreadsheets for management reports. Effective data manipulation.
Managerial	Improve presentation skills.	Practise by giving informal presentations in departmental meetings. Attend in-company presentations skills training course.	Able to prepare and deliver presentations to external departments and outside the company without assistance by the end of the year.

Figure 5.3 *Examples of developmental targets*

Developmental targets by definition serve the purpose of developing a skill, knowledge or ability in an area where it does not currently exist or, if it does, where there is room for improvement. The implications of this are that an individual might interpret the target in one of two ways, either as an implied or overt criticism of current ability or as an opportunity to develop and improve their repertoire of skills. This will depend very much on how the process of target setting is handled and the tone of the discussion between the manager and subordinate; this is discussed in the next chapter.

Success Criteria

You will notice that for the targets shown in Figure 5.3 there is a column headed 'success criteria'. The success criteria establish, at the target setting stage how it will be known at the review stage whether the target has been met or how well it has been met. By considering the subject of assessment at the start, review will be easier for both manager and subordinate and there is less likely to be disagreement because each had differing views of what was expected. It is especially important to build clear success criteria into developmental targets because it is less easy to include the type of numerical measure that is often found in quantitative targets. We will look at the subject of assessment in more detail in Chapter 6.

A useful approach when trying to determine success criteria for a particular target is to ask 'What should happen if the target is met?' The checklist in Figure 5.4 suggests a number of considerations which, if built in at the outset, will provide focus in working towards the target and help ease the process of assessment.

Method	Example
Cost	reduce costs to x
Speed	be able to operate at x speed
Deadlines	achieve the target in x months
Accuracy	achieve a certain level of accuracy
Number of mistakes	reduce the number of mistakes to x
Whether a task is achieved	has the job actually been done?
Knowledge level	knowledge can be tested
Skill level	observe someone doing it or test them
Change in behaviour	observe changed interpersonal skills
Amount of supervision needed	can they do the job alone?

Figure 5.4 *Methods of measurement – a checklist*

Top-down Support – Bottom-up Development

In a study of target setting in a number of organizations, Kane and Freeman (1986/7) identified three models of target setting: the democratic, the autocratic and the laissez-faire. This framework can help us think through some of the key issues in target setting generally and is summarized in Figure 5.5.

Target Setting in Practice

Autocratic Model	Top management decides on targets and imposes them downwards.
Democratic Model	Top management recommends targets which are agreed jointly with staff: target setting is a two-way process.
Laissez-faire Model	Top management has lost interest in the system and leaves managers to set what become vague targets.

Figure 5.5 *Three models of target setting*

Equally we could apply this model to all sorts of initiatives which might be introduced to an organization. If you know of target setting or performance appraisal schemes which have been introduced to an organization you might like to consider which model most accurately describes the way they were introduced.

Research has consistently shown that when there is participation in decision making regarding target setting from lower levels, useful information that is known to subordinates is passed upwards and decisions result in increased productivity. Senior level support for the target setting process is vital but participation is also critical in order to give credibility and an example or role model for others to follow (see Rogers and Hunter, 1991).

What we can learn from this is that on the one hand, managers should support and indeed become involved in the whole process of setting targets but, on the other, care should be taken to make sure subordinates have an input into deciding the subject matter and the success criteria of the targets they will be working towards. In the next chapter we look at the sequence of events in the target setting process and ways of ensuring employees have a real part to play in target setting.

Reinforcing Organizational Messages

We recommend that a set of targets for one person should focus on a maximum of six issues. Managers and individuals should attempt to identify the key areas of the job where achievement or improvement will have most impact. There should be a balance between targets which will contribute to organizational or departmental goals and those which develop the individual. This is where there is a real opportunity to ensure

The Practice of Target Setting

that targets will help both the person working towards the targets and his or her manager.

For example, if the department needs to improve communications with another, this rather vague aim can be brought down to a very practical level by identifying specific ways that one person can contribute to this departmental objective. This might be expressed in the following way:

> Improve communications with the site services department by involving their staff in our departmental meetings when appropriate and by increasing the amount of face-to-face contact through informal visits rather than relying so heavily on written memos.

Equally there may be overall organizational themes which can be reinforced through effective target setting. Some examples would be:

- improve awareness of company performance;
- improve service to customers;
- do not walk past poor quality;
- improve use of latest technology;
- present a certain image to external contacts;
- increase the level of effective communication both downwards and upwards;
- do more 'management by wandering around';
- reduce the amount of unnecessary paperwork.

By including a target which relates to an organizational concern it is possible to reinforce some of the key cultural messages and this is a particularly effective way of helping to introduce change in thinking and behaviour on a broad basis. Of course it is essential to ensure the messages are correct and there would need to be some lead from the most senior level in this respect.

The secret to introducing organizational change is to start by changing the behaviour of individuals and to ensure that on certain issues there is a measure of consistency. This will in turn provide role models for others and establish 'how things are done round here'. Others are then more likely to adjust or adopt appropriate attitudes, and so cultural norms are more easily established.

Using Targets to Breed Success

The term 'success criteria' referred to earlier is carefully and deliberately chosen. The emphasis is on individuals aiming to meet or exceed the target and the manager giving support for the same reason. All too often the focus is on *not* achieving the target and employees build up fears surrounding what will happen if the target is not met. What this means in terms of target setting is that every target should be achievable but stretching. This calls for careful judgement on the part of the trainer, the manager and the individual; obviously, what is easy for one person might be quite difficult for another. This will depend on a number of factors such as:

- experience
- existing knowledge
- enthusiasm
- fear
- confidence
- apparent relevance (face value)
- training
- education

Tom Peters (1989) sums up this subject perfectly in his book *Thriving on Chaos*:

> Put a 5 foot 10 inch person into 6 feet 3 inches of water, and odds are he'll learn to swim. He may sputter and spit a bit, but he can always hop up off the bottom and get air. Put that same person in 7 feet 4 inches of water and you may have a dead body on your hands.

It might feel slightly uncomfortable for the person trying to achieve the target but only by moving into new fields and pushing back the normal 'zone of comfort' will there be any real development. This is likely to lead to an upward cycle of success as shown in the lower section of Figure 5.6. If the

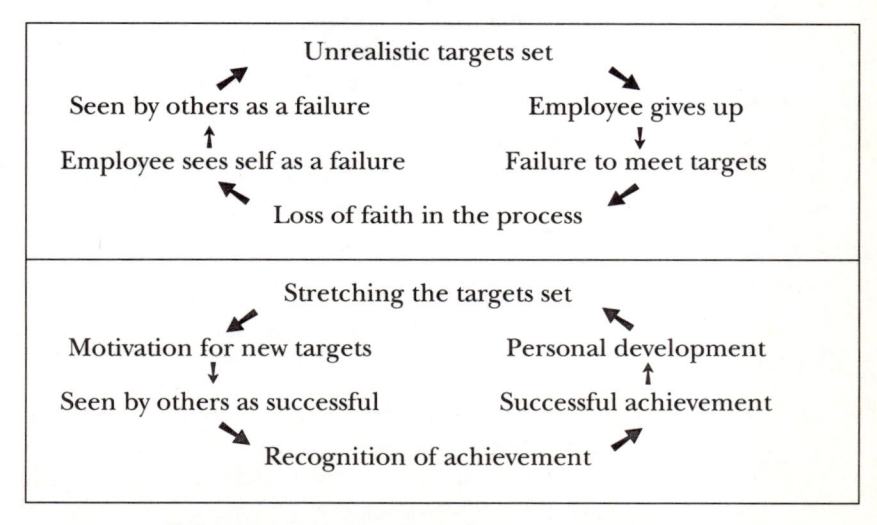

```
              Unrealistic targets set
         ↗                              ↘
Seen by others as a failure        Employee gives up
         ↑                              ↓
Employee sees self as a failure    Failure to meet targets
         ↖                              ↙
             Loss of faith in the process

              Stretching the targets set
         ↙                              ↖
Motivation for new targets         Personal development
         ↓                              ↑
Seen by others as successful       Successful achievement
         ↘                              ↗
             Recognition of achievement
```

Figure 5.6 *Setting achievable but stretching targets*

target is considered totally unachievable, however, it is likely to lead to a dead-end and failure as shown by the upper part of Figure 5.6.

How realistic the targets are will depend largely on the climate created by the manager and the organization. This is where the models explained earlier can help. If the climate suggested by the democratic model for target setting is created then it is quite likely that the individual will suggest over-ambitious success criteria or timescales and the managerial role is to tone them down to become more realistic and achievable.

If however, it is felt by employees that the system of target setting is purely a top-management mechanism for control, as suggested by the autocratic model, then employees are more likely to attempt to 'play the system' by ensuring that targets are set at an easily attainable level.

One way of creating a healthy climate is for the manager to demonstrate that the targets call for a two-way commitment: on the one hand the individual will work towards achievement of the target, on the other the manager will help the individual to achieve the target in whatever way possible. The checklist in Figure 5.7 provides examples of how the manager might help his or her staff work towards the achievement of a target.

- Coaching – for skills development
- Opening doors – facilitating senior level, specialist or external contacts
- Placements and secondments
- Freeing up time for prioritization of target area work
- Inclusion on circulation lists
- Sponsorship on training courses and conferences
- Mentoring
- Allocation of budgets
- Delegation of responsibility and authority
- Regular ongoing support and guidance

Figure 5.7 *Target setting as a two-way process – the manager's commitment*

There are no hard and fast rules regarding exactly how to word a target but as has been shown there are a number of ground rules which need to be applied to ensure that targets are realistically set and that they will prove motivating for the employee and beneficial for the organization. Appendix 2 (p111) provides examples of many targets for different job roles based on actual targets set in organizations which have realized the benefits of effective target setting.

> ### ACTIVITY
>
> Consider the following questions in relation to:
> - your own job;
> - your subordinate's job;
> - someone in a different department.
>
> In what areas of the job is it possible to set quantitative targets?
> What would be an appropriate developmental target?
> Try to write down these targets identifying output statements and success criteria.

6 Target Setting and Review

> SUMMARY <

In this chapter we will consider the review stage of the target setting initiative. It is suggested that a key to trouble free review of targets is to build standards and measures into the original targets at the design stage. We also suggest that it is important to consider links with the rewards system and to clarify the relationship between the targets and the whole job.

We offer a method for weighting targets and emphasize the importance of self review and continuous review. A model with recommended timescales is shown covering the various steps from target setting to review.

Trainers should ensure that the 'front end loaded' nature of the target setting process is understood throughout the organization, with the emphasis on establishing success criteria and means of assessment at the target setting rather than review stage. Trainers also need to encourage all employees to accept ownership for their targets and to see the potential benefits in terms of personal development rather than viewing target setting as a passive process which is imposed from the top down.

So far we have established the importance of laying the foundation for the successful implementation of target setting in an organization by identifying the links with existing human resource systems and anticipating the major functional and cultural implications. By anticipating the likely objections and hurdles to be overcome during implementation, success is more likely than by simply attempting to impose the system or importing a system from an external source. In the last chapter we looked at the specifics of how to set a target and some of the useful ground rules to ensure a target is measurable at the review stage. Here we will provide a framework and recommended timescale covering the full cycle from target setting through to the review stage including the vital interim steps.

Again there are a number of ground rules which are recommended and can be applied whatever the detailed nature of the procedures and paperwork of the organization. Review of progress against targets is often the most contentious and problematic aspect which those responsible for implementing target setting encounter and, as with the introduction of target setting, consideration of some of the common objections and pitfalls will help prepare the ground for success.

Preparation for Review when Targets are Set

The best advice with regards to the review stage suggests front-end loaded effort starting long before the review itself. By discussing the review of targets when actually setting them it is possible to clarify success criteria and to distinguish between unacceptable, acceptable and exceptional performance. Many individuals will feel that they are disadvantaged at the review stage by, for instance, the documentation which they have to use. Often they are quite justified in feeling that documentation could be improved and that it is constraining. It might be felt that if a review system requires a rating of, say, exceptional/acceptable/unacceptable then insufficient consideration is given to the details of performance against a target: managers simply tick a box based on fairly arbitrary judgement. For the manager and employee there is an effective way of working round such a system by describing at the target setting stage what the outcome might be for each of the ratings. Examples are given of how this might work in practice in Figure 6.1.

The subject of the target in this example is a managerial one which combines qualitative measures with a degree of quantitative assessment, but without overemphasis on numerical measures. When preparing for the target setting discussion both parties would benefit from thinking through these issues in advance. By asking the question 'What would be the circumstances and outcomes across a range of performance assessments?' the assessment process will be much more straightforward than if both parties make assumptions that the other person will be working from the same frame of reference and that there is no need to discuss assessment at such an early stage. Research by Locke and Latham (1990)

Subject of Target

For a manager to introduce a total quality management initiative which aims to improve communications and productivity over a period of one year.

Exceptional Performance

Performance will be considered exceptional if the total quality management initiative is fully embedded in the organization and a comparison of results for the site-wide attitude survey conducted at the start and end of the year reveals at least a doubling of positive responses against all four categories of question (commitment, training and development, human resource procedures and practices).

Furthermore a programme of associated training should be completed at supervisor and middle-management level and evidence should be provided that quality circles are self sustaining on at least three production lines and have progressed at least one successful idea each through to the implementation stage.

A random sample of staff will be expected to be able to explain satisfactorily key total quality management concepts and to quote the organization's mission statement.

Acceptable Performance

An improvement is identified when comparing the response to the employee attitude surveys.

Training programmes at supervisory and management level should have commenced and quality circles should have been established.

All staff should be aware of the organization's mission statement and in a random sample some should be able to explain the key concepts of total quality management.

Unacceptable Performance

There is no visible improvement in the response to the employee attitude survey.

> Training programmes will not have taken place and quality circles will not have been established or if they have, they will have been allowed to fall into disuse through lack of proper support.
>
> In a random sample of staff none will be able to explain satisfactorily the concepts of total quality management or will be aware of the organization's mission statement.

Figure 6.1 *Description of outcomes against a rating system*

found that in target setting there is normally a tendency to show leniency at the evaluation stage and this can be minimized if goals are defined in specific terms.

Balancing Targets with Other Responsibilities

The principle behind target setting is that by concentrating on the most important parts of the job, individuals will know where to apply effort which will make the most impact on the business. It was demonstrated by the nineteenth-century Italian economist Pareto that 80 per cent of the Italian population owned 20 per cent of the nation's wealth; it was discovered that this ratio could be applied in a number of different contexts. For instance 80 per cent of the costs of a product might be found in 20 per cent of the components or 80 per cent of the profits of an organization might come from just 20 per cent of its products or services. Similarly the Pareto principle might be applied to the job role and targets: 80 per cent of the impact an individual makes comes from just 20 per cent of the job responsibilities.

Selection of the target areas might be based on, for example

- linking the job to organizational objectives;
- developing managerial skills;
- developing interpersonal skills;
- improving ability to perform current tasks;
- preparing for the future;
- improving communications;
- broadening knowledge;
- achieving qualifications; or
- generating income, sales, fees, etc.

While it is important to attempt to identify the key 20 per cent of responsibilities, tasks or skill areas which will make 80 per cent of the impact it is equally critical to recognize that of the remaining 80 per cent there will be tasks or responsibilites, which, if ignored, will reflect on the overall ability of the employee, and could ultimately affect the tenability of the position. This suggests that while assessment should focus primarily on achievement of targets, credit should also be given for achievement in areas where targets are not established. If there is a job description this will identify the 'whole picture' in terms of areas of responsibility and targets to be achieved. Job descriptions, though, do not necessarily highlight the priorities and methods for meeting targets and deadlines; these need to be agreed on an individual basis through the target setting process.

Areas of the job which are not linked to targets but form an important part of the 80 per cent could include routine tasks, regular activities, aspects of work completed by a number of people and maintenance type responsibilities.

Remuneration schemes sometimes reward only achievement as judged against targets at the expense of ignoring other parts of the job. This can have a highly demotivational effect on those employees whose roles include a high degree of maintenance type activity. For such employees it may be appropriate to build some of the maintenance type activities into targets and to consider setting some common targets for a group of similar job holders, for example:

> Maintain an efficient filing system which enables ease and speed of access to current and accurate information by users.

> Demonstrate willingness to assist other operatives on their production line when your own line is not busy. Utilize assistance from operatives from other lines when your own line is particularly under pressure.

> Maintain a consistently courteous and helpful approach to customers and act upon their enquiries by promptly referring to the appropriate manager if you are unable to resolve issues alone.

Some organizations relate rewards to achievements through an annual or six-monthly bonus system and the achievement of the '80 per cent' type activities through the salary review. The emphasis in this sort of rewards system is on recognizing that if targets are achieved this demonstrates achievement over and above the baseline of expected responsibilities. In that continued achievement against these activities is not predictable in the future it is considered inappropriate to guarantee continual payment and to reward such achievement through the regular salary payments system. This can prove to be a motivational strategy but if this is at the expense of extrinsic recognition of efforts in the '80 per cent' type areas this can become a cause of dissent and dissatisfaction. The way that this is often handled is to include in the salary review an element which reflects continued good performance in the 80 per cent areas. This might form one element in the salary review calculation along with consideration of, for example, organizational results, trading conditions, local employment-market conditions, functional employment-market conditions and the current rate of inflation. The boxed exercise at the end of this chapter will help you to separate out these 80 per cent areas from other responsibilities.

Obviously reward systems vary considerably across organizations but it is critical to consider exactly how the achievement of results will be linked to rewards through remuneration in advance of, or in conjunction with, the implementation of a target setting initiative. In line with recent research (IPM, 1992) which has found that performance-related pay does not necessarily correlate with organizational bottom line results, some organizations are now repositioning the target setting and review process to distance it from pay reviews and rewards. This gives the advantage of being able to generate a more healthy two-way discussion about performance and personal development.

Sometimes it is obvious that while, say, six targets have been identified for a particular position, they do not all carry equal value in terms of either impact on the organization and individual or effort required to achieve them. In this case it is appropriate to prioritize and weight them accordingly. Weighting will depend on the relative values of issues such as:

- importance to the business, department, section;
- urgency, speed required;
- importance of personal development;
- imminence of future changes; and
- technological developments.

As with any weighting system it is possible to introduce sophisticated statistical techniques and the danger is that the system becomes an end in itself rather than a means to an end. A practical approach would be to rank each target area according to urgency and importance as in the worked example in Figure 6.2.

Twenty points to be distributed for importance and urgency across target subjects. 'Total' column is from a maximum of 40 points. 'Weighting' column is 'total' figure x 2.5 to give a total of 100 (per cent).

Target subject	Importance	Urgency	Total	Weighting
Develop a new admin system	1	4	5	12.5
Improve communications	6	6	12	30.0
Improve production methods	4	3	7	17.5
Form new project teams	5	1	6	15.0
Presentation skills	2	1	3	7.5
Recruit new team members	2	5	7	17.5
Total	20	20	40	100.0

Figure 6.2 *Weighting of targets*

The advantage of such a system is that there is agreement on the weighting and value of specific targets as early as the target setting stage. This means that employees will know where to focus their efforts and which targets to prioritize in terms of timescales once they have been set. Employees can then be given the discretion to decide on how to achieve their targets. This sort of weighting system also means that there will not be any surprises when it comes to the assessment of achievements with employees discovering that their managers had different views on the relevant importance of targets.

Encouraging Self Review and Continual Review

Just as it is fundamental in target setting to encourage employees to identify their own priorities when devising targets as a means of encouraging ownership, it is equally important to place the initial emphasis on the individual when reviewing progress and achievements. There are several advantages to beginning the review with the employee's reflections rather than passing judgement from on high.

First, the tone of the target setting initiative will be seen to be participative rather than autocratic and employees are far more likely to be committed to the agreement regarding outcomes and achievements. Second, it makes it much easier for managers to open up a constructive discussion on shortfalls or problem areas where targets have not been satisfactorily achieved. Interestingly most employees will be more critical of themselves than their manager would be and often the manager will have the more pleasant task of raising the self review in an upward direction. When the review process starts with the managers presenting their opinion of the performance of subordinates, there might be one of two potentially damaging reactions: there could be a heated and emotional disagreement, or, on the other hand the employee may feel less inclined to take issue with areas of disagreement and the opportunity for open discussion will be stifled.

It is also crucial to recognize that the review of targets is not a one-off and final event conducted at the end of the period for achievement. Employees should be encouraged to continually monitor their own progress against targets and the manager should conduct informal interim reviews throughout the period in question. This will mean that the emphasis of the final review is on finalizing and pulling together issues already discussed in interim reviews.

If there have been interim reviews and a continual discussion of progress towards targets with ongoing support from management in helping the employee to achieve them then unpleasant suprises at the final review are less likely. Continual review also provides the opportunity to agree modifications to targets if it is accepted that the original parameters have changed significantly due to circumstances beyond the employee's control and the target has become inappropriate or unrealistic.

Timescales from Target Setting to Review

When setting targets there is a danger that, in considering deadlines, all the targets will be set to be achieved by the major review date, that is usually after six or twelve months. The problem with this approach is that the employee will find that as the date for review looms there are a number of major activities which have been put off and overall success is less likely than if dates for completion of targets had been spread throughout the year. When deciding on the priority of targets it will be apparent in considering the aspect of urgency and demands on the employee that some targets can be set for completion earlier than others.

At an organizational level it is necessary to decide whether the main review of targets is going to be held for all staff at the same time of year or at different times for each employee. Clearly the advantages of linking review to individually related dates, such as the anniversary of commencing employment or birthdays will spread the administrative load on the organization and departmental managers fairly evenly throughout the year. This also will help to encourage the view that the review of targets is a continual process which should be built into the everyday activities of management. By reviewing targets at the same time of year for all employees, however, it is more likely that, due to the pressure this puts on managers in coping with the sheer number of reviews to be completed, the process will be considered more administrative than developmental.

Another advantage of spreading reviews for employees throughout the year is that they will be less likely to place quite so much emphasis on comparing the results of their own review with those of their peers. This will mean that more valuable judgements can be drawn as the individual compares performance and achievements against previous skills and abilities.

Figure 6.3. shows a schematic for covering recommended timescales for the entire process from target setting through to summary review. Obviously precise timescales will vary between organizations but the schematic suggests some key stages.

Figure 6.3 suggests that the first stage of the entire process should be an introductory discussion between the manager and the subordinate to explain the aims of target setting and the system as operated in the organization. At this stage it is necessary to explain the order of the target setting process and to show the subordinate the associated documentation and how it will be used. Both parties should finally agree to consider broad subject areas which will form the basis for more detailed discussion and development of targets. Ideally both the manager and subordinate will have had some training in the skills of target setting before reaching this stage but in reality this is not always the case. If there has been no training for the subordinate then it will be helpful for the manager to provide a briefing and if responsible for a group of staff then a workshop for the departmental team can be a useful way of generating a discussion and a full understanding of the most important issues. The subject of training and target setting skills is covered in Chapter 8.

A reasonable time lapse between the original discussion and the main target setting meeting is about two weeks. This will enable the subordinate to become more familiar with the process and the documentation

Activity	Timing	Objective
Introductory discussion; manager and subordinate		Outline aims of target setting Benefits to individual and organization Paperwork involved Both agree to consider key areas for targets
	2 weeks	
Main target setting meeting		Discuss and decide on broad target areas
	1 week	
Completion of written documentation by manager and subordinate		
Signing off of targets		Final agreement of targets Clarification of two-way commitment Manager to explain how subordinate will be helped Subordinate to agree to work towards targets Agree timescales
Continued monitoring and review of targets	6 months	
Summary review		Summary review of achievement against targets Forward planning of future targets
	2 days	
Signing off reviewed targets		Confine agreement with review

Figure 6.3 *Schematic of the target setting process*

and to give sufficient serious thought to target areas which will be of personal as well as departmental and organizational benefit. It may also be appropriate to refer upwards to the manager during this pre-target setting period to discuss ideas on subjects for targets. Even when this does not occur it is surprising how often both parties will identify similar areas upon which to base targets.

The next stage is for the target setting meeting to take place and sufficient time should be allocated for a constructive discussion on level terms. A suggested structure for this meeting is to start by agreeing the six or so subjects which will form the basis of separate targets; here it is possible to check that there is a balance between different types of target such as technical, managerial, personal, developmental and organizational. On comparing target subjects it is likely that some suggested subjects can be linked with others in an attempt to reduce the number of targets to a maximum of around six.

The next stage of the discussion should focus on defining success criteria, timescales and how the manager will help the subordinate to achieve the targets agreed. Some managers like to complete the relevant documentation at this stage, while others prefer to do this outside the context of the target setting meeting. The major drawback of completing documentation during the meeting is that free-flowing conversation tends to be cramped as paperwork takes over.

Allowing a short period of time between the meeting and the completion of the documentation will also provide the employee with the opportunity to think about the targets which have been discussed without feeling under pressure. Providing the opportunity for subsequent refinement of targets before finally signing them off also helps to encourage ownership.

When actually signing off the relevant documentation it should be made clear that both parties are entering into a two-way commitment; the employee will work towards the target and the manager will make resources and expertise available to help.

The ongoing review meetings which can be carried out at, say, monthly intervals do not need to be extended discussions. If there is continual informal support and review of progress then these will simply be a discussion of views, problems and plans for progressing towards the individual targets. For the manager this is clearly another occasion where assistance can be offered to facilitate success for the subordinate.

The final review is really a summary of all reviews to date and an overall discussion of success as measured against the original criteria. It also coincides with the timing of the development of new targets, some of which will be identified as evolving naturally from the old ones.

Again the principle of allowing some time before signing the overall review will allow the employee to consider, alone, whether the review as discussed at the meeting is fair and it will allow time for completion of relevant company review documents.

> ### DISTINGUISHING TARGETS FROM OTHER RESPONSIBILITIES
>
> 1. Starting with a job description if you have one, or starting from afresh, list all the tasks and responsibilities which feature in your job.
> 2. Categorize these into goals, key areas, and specific tasks.
> 3. Draw out subjects which you consider important enough to form the basis for targets and list these again separately.
> 4. Add to the original list of targets additional subjects for targets by considering the future of the job and the organization and your own development needs to achieve personal goals.
>
> You should now have separated key targets, that is the 20 per cent of your responsibilities which will generate 80 per cent of the impact.

7 The Interpersonal Skills of Target Setting and Review

> ▷ **SUMMARY** ◁
>
> In this chapter we focus on the communication skills which need to be developed in order to cope with the interpersonal aspects of target setting and review. The trainer should be continually seeking to develop the interpersonal skills of employees through direct training interventions and informal methods such as coaching, briefings and the provision of information. In particular we consider:
>
> - listening;
> - feedback;
> - empathy;
> - questioning; and
> - confrontation.
>
> We then look at how perception becomes distorted and how this can affect judgement of performance. The trainer should raise the awareness of this subject amongst employees and is in a strong position to open discussion where evidence of perceptual distortion is seen.

There are a number of interpersonal skills which need to be practised and developed when setting targets with staff. Refining some of these skills is a subtle and continuous process which will come with experience and effort it is possible to identify the basic components of such skills and consciously to develop them through a structured approach to on- and off-job training. For the trainer the challenge is to facilitate the development of these skills throughout the organization through a combination of formalized training interventions and continual coaching.

The specific interpersonal skills we will look at here can be applied in several managerial contexts but are especially relevant when it comes to target setting and reviewing progress against targets. Ironically they tend to be the communication skills which we have to practise earliest in our development and use the most but are not taught as part of our general education. We will consider the skills of listening and questioning and how we can combine these to convey an empathetic and objective approach to target setting and review. We will also identify the component parts of effective feedback, which are of particular relevance to the target review process. It is also important to be aware of some of the natural human failings we are susceptible to in processing information, making judgements about others and the various ways in which our perception tends to become distorted. By developing an understanding of our limitations and prejudices and adjusting behaviour accordingly it is possible to take a more objective approach which is the key to successful target setting and review.

Communication Skills

Target setting should be positioned clearly as a two-way communication process involving the manager and subordinate and as such there are a number of potential blocks to effective communication which should be avoided to ensure maximum gain is experienced by both parties. It is particularly important to consider the nature of the communication process as it involves a superior/subordinate relationship and the intention is to discuss what is actually a very personal subject. The danger with target setting and review is that the discussion revolves around the technical aspects of the job or task and a work-centred discussion ensues rather than one focusing on how the individual will achieve the target. The task-centred rather than person-centred approach is especially likely to occur when the nature of the industry or job is technical and it is relatively easy to avoid the difficult aspect of discussing personal performance which usually means dealing with emotion and sometimes handling conflict and confrontation.

There are some commonsense suggestions which will ease the communication process and are more likely to encourage open discussion; these are covered in the checklist in Figure 7.1.

The Practice of Target Setting

Environment	Noise, seating, heating, lighting, interruptions.
Timing	Keep to the agreed date, time of day, time of week, amount of time.
Assumptions	Level of knowledge, level of skill, confidence, attitude.
Prejudices	Assuming others will feel the same as us, our own strengths are not necessarily those of others.
Status	Be aware of the status relationships.
Value Others	Everyone has a right to their own views.
Non-verbal	Back up words with the appropriate non-verbal communication, tone, posture, expressions.
Verbal	Be aware of value judgements, and emotionally charged words, eg 'brilliant', 'hopeless'.
Withholding Information	Question whether it needs to be withheld.
Confrontation	Do not avoid it, channel it constructively.
Listening	Practise active listening.
Questioning	Use questions to demonstrate listening.
Empathy	Put yourself in the other person's shoes.
Silence	Do not fear silence, use it effectively, allow thinking time.
Feedback	Give constructive feedback.

Figure 7.1 *Checklist for improving communications in target setting and review*

There are a number of issues here which the manager needs to consider, both in target setting and review. In the worst scenario the target setting interview or the target review interview takes place as something fitted in among other supposedly more important pressures and the meeting is subject to interruptions and is often rearranged for another time. This marginalizes what to the individual is a very important activity.

It is worth considering the most appropriate time of day for the discussion: this will differ across organizations but managers should try to find a time which will allow for overrun if necessary. It is easy for the manager to make incorrect assumptions about how a task is viewed by the subordinates regarding, for example, degree of difficulty and confidence in approaching it. It is a mistake to steamroll the imposition of a target. It is important to show empathy with employees and to find out how they feel about a particular subject and to attempt to summarize their underlying feelings both when setting targets and when reviewing them.

It should be recognized that as the target setting and review interviews are usually coordinated by managers with their subordinates that there may be natural barriers which inhibit free-flowing conversation. This problem can be countered by creating a climate of mature and constructive conversation rather than judgement from above. On occasions it will be necessary to accept that confrontation, however, is inevitable and indeed requisite. If an employee has clearly not performed then this cannot be ignored at the review stage. If there has been regular ongoing conversation about performance on an informal basis throughout the year then there is less likely to be confrontation as there will be few surprises for the employee being reviewed. When there are disagreements though, the manager should attempt to identify the root cause; it may be the case that the employee being reviewed has information, previously unknown to the manager, as to why targets were not met.

Some of the specific skills worth developing in more depth are those of listening, empathizing, questioning and giving feedback.

Listening

As an interpersonal skill listening is often confused with hearing. It is possible, for instance, to hear background music without thinking about the words being sung or their meaning. This is different to listening actively which is a skill we can consciously develop. People avoid listening for a variety of reasons; for instance it may be that we do not hear what we do not want to hear. This is a defence mechanism which helps us avoid a problem or reality. This has serious implications in the context of reviewing progress against targets for both the manager and the subordinate being reviewed. Both parties may not actually understand what the other party is saying. It is also common for people to avoid listening when the other person's views contradict their own ideas and preconceptions. This again presents a number of dangers when reviewing targets. Also it is natural to avoid listening due to information overload; in other words it is just not possible to think about all the issues being discussed at once. Listening skills can actually be broken down into specific techniques; some of these are explained in Figure 7.2.

Technique	Example
Non-verbal communication	Head nod, tone, eye contact, facial expression.
Summarizing	'So in summary you believe you have achieved the target for the following reasons …'
Repeating key words	Echoing back key words and generating more output from the speaker.
Encouragement	'That is very interesting, tell me more …', 'Mmm', 'Uh-huh'.
Reflect back feelings	'So you are clearly pleased with your performance'.
Pauses	Silence can be used to buy time in which to prepare thoughts and allow the other person to think through responses; establish from early on that silence is acceptable.

Figure 7.2 *Active listening techniques*

One of the most difficult and advanced aspects of active listening is showing empathy. This really means understanding not just how a person feels but why they feel like they do. By demonstrating empathy when reviewing targets it is much more likely that constructive conversation will follow. Showing empathy does not mean talking about yourself or attempting to impose solutions. It is about listening to, and understanding, the other person's position and feelings before offering ideas and working towards solutions.

In the empathizing exercise shown you might like to offer an empathetic response to the three comments made by the employee who is being reviewed against the achievement of targets.

The responses suggested in the example may sound contrived and obviously there are many ways of offering an empathetic response, but the principle is important: demonstrate your understanding of the underlying feelings before moving on to proposed solutions or making judgements.

EMPATHIZING WHEN REVIEWING TARGETS

Rephrase the following statements from the person you are reviewing to give an empathetic response which shows that you recognize and understand their underlying feelings.

1. It has just not been possible to achieve the target this year because of the problems with changing workload, the fact that my job role has increased due to losing staff. I never get a chance to concentrate on any one thing. I get pushed about by top management all the time and I have just about had enough.

2. It's great; this time last year I would never have thought that I could achieve so much and that I would be mixing with our customers on a regular basis. It is really exciting to be the main representative of the company at social events and I really get a buzz out of the public relations aspect of the job.

3. I never get consulted about the new recruits who join this section. The way I get to find out about anything is through gossip in the corridor and even then I am the last to hear. It seems everyone else knows what's happening. How do you expect me to meet targets if you do not let me know what is going on?

Examples of Inappropriate Responses

1. I know. I get fed up with the never-ending changes too. I don't know whether I am coming or going sometimes.
(Inappropriate response because it focuses on the reviewer rather than the reviewee.)

2. You are clearly going places.
(Inappropriate response because it moves the conversation on with an assumption about the future.)

3. Why don't you stop moaning and take a more positive outlook or you will never get anywhere.
(Inappropriate response because it moves into the problem-solving stage without involving the other person; it suggests a solution.)

Examples of Empathetic Responses

1. It sounds like you are quite angry because of the changes which have been imposed on you.

2. You seem very pleased with the increased responsibilities you have been given.

3. It must be very frustrating to feel left out when it comes to communication about changes in staffing.

Questioning

Just as listening is a vital skill which will come to the fore at the target setting and review stages, the skills of effective questioning are equally important. Effective questioning techniques can help when it comes to discussing potential target areas and when reviewing progress. The most useful types of question here are those that encourage self review and draw on ideas from the individual rather than impose the views of the manager. Figure 7.3 gives some examples which might be appropriate in target setting and review.

Target Setting

1. What do you consider to be the most important aspects of your job?
2. What help do you need to ensure that you succeed in the future?
3. How could you measure your success?
4. In what ways is your role changing?
5. What are the external influences on your performance?
6. What are your special interest areas?
7. What technical aspects of your job are important?
8. What skills do you need to help you develop further?
9. What knowledge do you need to acquire?
10. What qualifications would help you for the future?
11. What are your short-term priorities and what are your medium and long-term goals?

Target Review

1. How do you feel that you have performed against this target?
2. What areas are you pleased with?
3. What areas are you disappointed with?
4. What helped you to achieve this target?
5. How do you feel about the level of cooperation you have received when working towards this target?
6. In what ways has the target helped you to develop personal skills?
7. What technical skills have you developed?
8. What knowledge do you have now that you did not have before?
9. What do you consider to be your strengths/weaknesses?

Figure 7.3 *Examples of questions to ask when setting and reviewing targets*

Feedback

Having encouraged self review of performance against targets by the employee, the manager will need to offer feedback. Giving feedback is a skill in itself and there are a number of guidelines which need to be adhered to. Feedback should describe effective or ineffective behaviour rather than consist of sweeping generalizations or evaluative statements.

For example it is more appropriate to state 'You have worked closely with your team and helped to integrate new members through the instigation of team meetings', than to say 'Great teamwork!' Similarly, rather than saying 'You are a hopeless leader', a more effective approach would be 'Your team leadership has suffered because you have not given sufficient time and emphasis to group activities utilizing your staff'.

Effective feedback specifies or describes the behaviour and should focus on things that are capable of being modified. So, for example, it would be inappropriate to criticize an employee for failing to carry out a physical task fast enough if they are physically incapable of doing so. At a more subtle level the manager should be sensitive to the less obvious limitations of the individual.

Confrontation

Inevitably there will be occasions when the individual has a perception of their own performance different from the manager and there may be confrontation. Clearly this will be less likely if the targets have been set according to the principles discussed earlier. When it does occur, though, confrontation needs to be managed and both parties should make explicit their own view and clarify differences in opinion. A useful procedure to follow when facing a confrontation situation is to:

1. accept that the other person currently has a different view;
2. identify the differences from your own view;
3. actively listen to check that you have understood correctly the other person's views – use rephrasing and summarizing techniques;
4. recognize the feelings in the other person; show empathy. Watch out for anger which tends to be accompanied by faster, louder or higher-pitched speech or aggressive language and posture;
5. recognise your own feelings and emotions; name them but differentiate feelings from facts;
6. do not move into attempting to solve the problem until differences on both sides have been discussed;

7 ask the other person to suggest some preferred solutions, and state your own; aim for a workable compromise.

There are, then, a number of techniques and skills which the effective manager needs to develop in order to be able to maximize the benefits of target setting and review. It is also helpful to be aware of ways in which our perception of others can be distorted; it is then possible to guard against these tendencies and maintain as objective and fair an approach as possible.

Perceptual Distortions

Attraction to Like

There is a natural tendency to be attracted to others who are similar to ourselves. Similarities might include, for example, appearance, common interests, strengths, background, gender, race, hobbies and sports. The danger here is that we confuse liking someone with making an objective appraisal of their performance.

Halo and Horns Effect

There is a natural tendency to assume that if someone succeeds in one aspect of their life or behaviour they must be successful in all other areas of their life. Similarly if someone has failed in one area then we often assume that they will do so in every other respect. We place a figurative halo or a set of horns on their heads, hence the use of phrases such as 'black sheep', 'blue-eyed boy', and 'golden girl'. In evaluating performance it is important to measure achievement against the specific criteria originally agreed and not to fall into the trap of making assumptions based on irrelevant data or information.

Stereotypes

We are all susceptible to the dangers of stereotyping: making assumptions that a lot of other characteristics follow on from one aspect of a person's character. We fit people into the stereotypical image for that category of person. Stereotypes are based around a number of issues such as gender, race, religion, age and profession or occupation. It is, however, possible to make serious misjudgements about people because of the tendency to stereotype. Some examples of stereotypical assumptions are:

- women are less capable than men of performing physical duties;
- older people will not accept change;
- young people will enjoy lively activity;
- accountants are serious and conservative;
- manual workers cannot contribute to management decisions;
- the family man is not ambitious;
- marketing people are aggressive;
- religious people are calm and contented.

Looking at these statements logically it is obvious that we cannot and should not make such sweeping generalizations. It is particularly dangerous to make such judgements when considering what targets to set for staff and when evaluating performance against targets. Assessment must be based on observable and justifiable evidence.

Primacy and Recency Effect

In terms of the human memory and impressions, there is a tendency to be disproportionately affected by first impressions and the most recent event; these perceptual distortions are known as the primacy and recency effect. The implications when monitoring performance are that the manager may fail to review the whole period since the target was set and instead focus on, for instance, the initial teething problems or honeymoon period or the most recent success or failure.

ACTIVITY

Consider the performance of a member of staff or colleague and formulate a plan for giving effective feedback in an area where there is room for improvement or development.

Consider your own prejudices and the stereotypes which you are susceptible to. A useful way of approaching this is to recall when you say 'He or she is a typical ...'

Who do you know of in your organization who benefits from the halo effect or is a victim of the horns effect?

III

Training in Target Setting and Target Achievement

III

8 Training Managers and Employees to Set Targets

> ▷ SUMMARY ◁
>
> In this chapter we consider the importance of training when introducing target setting to an organization. Two examples of training intervention are shown; the half-day workshop, and the two-day off-job training course. We consider who to involve in training and methods of providing ongoing support beyond the initial training programme. Trainers need to judge the method and depth of training which is appropriate for their organization and the two examples shown here are simply meant to provide ideas of different approaches. Trainers can also play a key role in the involvement of senior managers in supporting training.

In Part I we considered the importance of viewing target setting in the historical context of developments in the field of performance management and we stressed the importance of recognizing the existing systems and the culture of the organization before attempting to introduce a target setting programme. In Part II we looked at the practicalities of target setting, that is how to set and review targets at an individual level and the relevance of core interpersonal skills.

It is now relevant to look at how to introduce target setting to the organization. Clearly it is self defeating for the human resource or training specialist simply to design a system and impose it on the organization. It is essential to launch target setting with appropriate training which will serve two key purposes. First, training should address the subject of how target setting links with other related systems such as performance appraisal and performance-related pay. This also means that coverage of the practical steps of target setting is necessary. This will include the use of documentation, the reporting and monitoring system and timescales. Second, it is essential to offer the opportunity for practice and development of the key interpersonal skills identified in Chapter 7 and practice in designing example targets which conform to the ground rules for effective targets.

Focusing on these two issues, the system and the skills, will pave the way for successful implementation by enabling managers to raise their major concerns in the constructive forum of a training course or workshop. It is important to recognize these concerns from an early stage in order to help encourage managers to buy into the process. Development of knowledge and skills in target setting is in fact the easier part of training, whereas the development of appropriate attitudes is a longer-term project which must start at the launch stage.

Clearly there will be a cost associated with training in target setting and the options used by organizations range from the one-week residential programme through to half-day workshops on site, each with their associated scale of costs. Such costs need to be weighed against the projected costs of not training. For example without training there are likely to be high costs in terms of dealing with managers on an individual basis to tackle problems as and when they arise, and the costs of coping with the fact that managers are likely to apply target setting in an inconsistent manner without training and the costs of dealing with staff who may become demotivated by what they perceive as a poorly implemented system.

Provision of target setting can be approached in two stages: first the design of training and second the implementation of training. We will look at these aspects of training by suggesting two different types of training input: the short workshop and the off-job course. We will look at these in terms of method, timing and content.

The decision on the amount and type of training necessary will be determined by consideration of previous training given, existing skills and anticipation of attitudes towards target setting. If there has been a history of successful performance appraisal and the target setting initiative is simply intended to enhance the existing system, then it may be appropriate to provide short practical workshops on the site of the organization. On the other hand if the organization has a history of performance appraisal and monitoring which has not been successful then overcoming attitude barriers may be a major issue. In this case it is often more appropriate to take managers off site for a residential programme over a period of at least two days. In terms of who designs and delivers training, again there are a number of choices. Players in target setting training might include training and development staff, personnel professionals, line managers and senior managers and external consultants. It may be relevant to involve all these parties in different capacities. At the design stage trainers should project-manage the development of training, drawing on other expertise from the personnel function and if possible involving line managers. It may be the case that external consultants are able to offer a breadth of experience and specialist expertise in performance management, but simply buying in 'off the shelf' training and performance appraisal systems without tailoring them to the needs of the organization is a sure way to generate problems at the implementation stage. A very powerful technique is to involve representatives from senior management in providing an input to training. This might take the form of an introductory input to explain from a senior-management perspective where target setting sits within the context of organizational goals and objectives.

At the design stage it is also crucial to consider how those who will not be involved in setting targets for others, but will be on the receiving end of target setting, will be trained. Options here include specific training for employees falling into this category or integration of such staff with managers and supervisors for training programmes which are covered on a department-by-department basis. A common mistake is to focus only on those who are setting targets for others. This is often at the expense of the person who is actually going to work towards achievement of the target. This is likely to engender a 'them and us' feeling and unlikely to generate a positive attitude towards target setting from the start.

Shown below are the two examples of training intervention. Obviously there are a number of other options available in terms of length of training and detailed content but the examples below show the two different approaches, the on-job and the off-job input.

Model for an On-site Target Setting Workshop

Objectives

To introduce the target setting initiative to managers and their staff so that they understand how the current system of performance appraisal has been developed to include target setting.

To develop target setting skills and provide an understanding of the ground rules relating to target setting.

Training in Target Setting

Method

Facilitation of a three-hour workshop by a training officer with the use of lecture, handouts and group exercises in target setting.

Timetable

Time	Content and Method
9.00	Introduction to target setting initiative and the workshop.
9.15	Understanding of exsisting performance appraisal system – problems, pitfalls, benefits. Guided discussion.
9.45	Guidance on target setting through lecture and handouts (see Appendix 2, p111, for examples of handouts which could be used in this way). Delegates are asked to identify a subject for target setting which could be for their own job, their manager's job, their subordinate's job and practise the design of targets in pairs for presentation to the group.
10.15	Presentation of model targets to the group which will decide whether they meet the criteria established in the previous session. Group discussion.
11.00	Documentation and system issues such as timescale from target setting to review and the role of the personnel department. Explanation of follow-up support which is available for managers and provided by the personnel and training departments. Input with handouts.
11.30	Review of the workshop with an open forum for questions and answers. Action planning for target setting by departmental and sectional managers.
12.00	Close

Model for an Off-job Residential Training Course

Objectives

To provide the opportunity for open discussion of target setting. To develop positive attitudes towards target setting and willingness among delegates to participate in the organization's target setting initiative after the training programme has been completed.

To develop the interpersonal skills associated with effective target setting and review and to increase knowledge of how to set targets.

Method

A two-day off-site training course which is coordinated and tutored by the training department with inputs from the personnel manager and the managing director. The course combines discussion, lectures and participative exercises. Delegates receive a briefing on course objectives and a timetable one week before attending the course.

Timetable

Time	Content and Method
DAY ONE	
9.00	Introduction to course content, objectives, style and methods. Discussion of hopes, fears and expectations for the course and the target setting initiative facilitated by the course leader.
9.45	Exercise in syndicate groups to consider how performance is currently measured and in what ways staff are given future direction. Followed up by plenary discussion.
10.45	Lecture on developments in the field of performance management supplemented with handouts and discussion.
11.45	Lecture and discussion on developments in the organization's performance-management system. Delivered by the personnel manager.
12.30	Lunch
1.30	Skills development exercises in syndicates facilitated by group tutors. Coverage of questioning skills, listening skills and feedback skills.
4.00	Lecture and discussion on the techniques of target setting, including ground rules for effective target setting and discussion of how targets can be set in specialist areas, eg technical, creative, service and administration functions (see Appendix 2, p111, for examples of handouts which could be used here).
4.30	Preparation for target setting exercise which will be conducted on day two. Delegates identify three different types of targets for their own position or their staff's – organizational, developmental and functional. Sharing of thoughts with other delegates.
5.30	Close

Training in Target Setting

DAY TWO

9.00	Review of learning points from day one. Discussion facilitated by course tutor.
9.30	Preparation, in pairs, of targets by delegates. Exercise with guidance and support from tutors.
11.00	Presentation of targets to the plenary group by delegates. Delegates present their targets on flipcharts.
12.30	Lunch
1.30	Target setting in context – performance appraisal video. Video which demonstrates the application of target setting and performance appraisal in other organizations. (See Appendix 4 for a list of recommended videos.)
2.00	Question and answer forum with senior management guest. Managing director or senior manager to chair a panel to field questions with the personnel manager.
3.00	Action planning session where delegates plan how and when they will implement target setting in their own departments. At this stage commitment will be made for local training in departments.
4.00	Course review to discuss feedback on the training course and for completion of course evaluation and debriefing documents.
4.30	Close

The two models presented above serve to illustrate that the approach to training will be determined in part by existing knowledge and skills as well as attitudes of managers. If there is likely to be a high level of resistance to target setting then the in-depth approach suggested by the two-day course will be more appropriate. Moving away from the workplace and giving more time to training is likely to open up objective discussion once managers have been able to air grievances and concerns through the catharsis which will probably occur on the first day. These issues will need to be heard and dealt with professionally. This will reduce the likelihood of accusations of the organization imposing the initiative on employees under duress.

Having provided training it is of vital importance to offer ongoing support to managers. It is frequently the case that we fall into the trap of assuming that because the managers have attended the training course they are sufficiently trained and confident to continue without further support. In fact it is not quite so simple: development extends beyond initial training and the skills of setting and reviewing targets will continue to be developed and refined with experience.

It is constructive to build on the real experience of setting targets and use such material to identify good practice and areas for continual development. Possible methods are for the training officer or personnel specialist to be sent copies of targets once they are set and to consider how well they meet the requirements of effective targets; are they specific, measurable, achievable and timebound? Including the human resource specialist on the circulation list for targets once they have been set enables records to be held and used for the purpose of, for example, training provision, succession planning and, not least of all, monitoring the effectiveness of the target setting initiative.

Methods of follow up might include one-to-one coaching or short, focused workshops. It is also a powerful technique to identify examples of good-quality targets and circulate sample copies in order to reinforce the success of target setting throughout the organization. Obviously it might be necessary to depersonalize such targets in order to preserve confidentiality.

ACTIVITY

Consider the implementation of target setting in your own organization.
- Who should and could be invited in as a senior management representative to support the initiative?
- In what way could such representatives be used to help in a training course?
- What methods and type of training would you consider appropriate for your organization?

9 How to Achieve Targets through Visualization

> ▷   SUMMARY   ◁
>
> In this chapter we consider how it is possible for employees to improve their chances of successfully achieving targets by using our understanding of the 'self-fulfilling prophecy' concept and by the method known as visualization.
>
> Research (Alder, 1991) has shown that by imprinting images of the outcome required in their mind, individuals can enhance the likelihood of achievement.

Self-fulfilling Prophecy

Considerable research (Shone, 1984; Gallwey, 1986a, b) in the past into the psychology behind success has demonstrated the practicality of the self-fulfilling prophecy concept. Parents and adults make broad judgements about children when they are very young: comments such as 'She is not an academic' and 'He is very talented at sports'. Having been judged by several influential people the child eventually repeats 'I am not an academic' or 'I am good at sports'. The message originally suggested by others is taken on board by the children. As they grow up they behave in a way that continues to reinforce such judgements, for example by ignoring or shying away from academic study or devoting time to sporting activity, and the original prophecy is gradually fulfilled.

The same principle can be applied to the development of employees in terms both of developing others and of individuals developing themselves. The danger of the manager labelling an employee as successful or unsuccessful is most real. If the initial judgement is that 'the face doesn't fit' then the manager will react primarily to any evidence which supports such judgement and the individuals, believing 'they do not fit in', will be increasingly wary about even trying to. This is the downside of the self-fulfilling prophecy concept. Equally it can work in a positive way. For newly promoted supervisors who begin to hear from their staff or management that they are good at managing people, such encouragement will lead to positive reinforcement and continued success will ultimately lead to a good reputation. By this stage the reputation actually becomes quite difficult to live down and the supervisors are likely to feel obliged to do everything they can to live up to it.

Visualization

Another very practical application of psychology to the achievement of targets is the concept of visualization. This is the secret behind the success of many great athletes. They identify their target, then as they work towards it, they actually imprint images in their minds of the outcome and speak positively in interviews about how they know they will succeed whether this means to run the fastest, win the game or achieve gold. They picture the event several times in their minds and see themselves on the rostrum at the victory ceremony. This ability to visualize the ultimate achievement is a characteristic of some of the most successful sporting and business personalities alike. Experiments in the sporting field have shown that the mental 'tryout' is a practical way of improving ability; by practising netting the ball mentally, basketball players were able to achieve similar levels of improvement to those who practised physically. Both categories performed significantly better than those who did not practise at all (see Maltz, 1986).

Peter Whitlam (1993) has researched the application of such concepts to the field of management. There are some specific techniques which employees can apply when working towards targets. By actually writing the goal down as an affirmation it is possible to start programming the subconscious to visualize the achievement of the desired target. Having written down the affirmation it is possible to imprint it by creating visual images of the outcome. Here it is possible to tap into the under-utilized creative right side of the brain by thinking through the success in pictures and colours and by trying to imagine the feelings of success. Examples of affirmations and how they relate to targets are shown in Figure 9.1.

Target Area	Affirmation
Develop closeness to the customers	'I treat all my internal and external customers as if they were my only customers; I feel good when they recognize the service I am giving.'
Improve filing	'I keep filing up to date so that information can be found quickly; this means that I am seen as a helpful contact in the organization.'
Develop communication skills	'I enjoy communicating effectively through expressive speech and strong concise written notes which keep my staff up to date with developments.'

Figure 9.1 *Targets and affirmations*

You will note that the example affirmations are written in the present tense as though the target has been achieved and they are all worded in a positive way and in the first person; the focus is very much on the individual working towards the target rather than other people and where possible the emotion associated with successful achievement of a target is identified.

Such techniques can be applied to develop individuals once targets have been set as part of the organization's target setting or performance appraisal initiatve. Equally by experimenting with visualization and affirmations, individuals may discover an approach to self development which they wish to practise as part of their own personal agenda.

ACTIVITY

Think of three personal targets you would like to achieve over the next six months.

Write these down as an affirmation – in the present tense and first person and identify the emotion associated with success.

Read these affirmations twice a day as you work towards the target and practise mentally by visualizing the successful outcomes.

Appendix 1

Higgins and Duke Case Study – Chapter 2 – Possible Answers

It should have been made obligatory for Tom to have had at least some form of performance appraisal training. This may have included coaching if he felt particularly threatened by the idea of a traditional off-job course.

Ernest should have spoken to Tom personally in advance of the meeting in order to agree the dates of the appraisal meeting and to discuss the format. This should not have been handled through the secretary.

The meeting date once fixed should have been adhered to. Cancelling the meeting only served to devalue its importance in the eyes of Tom. In this case it seems that Monday morning was not a good time of the week to arrange such a meeting.

During the meeting there was clearly a problem with paperwork constraining the flow of conversation. The discussion should have been balanced approximately 70/30 in Tom's favour rather than Ernest as the appraiser dominating the discussion.

It was also hinted that Ernest may have simply been passing on the issues discussed at his own performance appraisal interview to Tom. Clearly the focus should have been on Tom and his performance.

The tick-box system was not known to Tom. It should have been, and the style of the interview was very much judgemental rather than one of joint problem solving. In addition the good grades which Tom was awarded were given grudgingly rather than Ernest taking the opportunity to celebrate and recognize areas of success.

Tom was required to sign off the form at the end of the meeting rather than being given the opportunity to consider the content of the discussion. A more suitable approach would have been to give him time to think about the discussion and raise any queries or concerns at a later stage.

Appendix 2

Handouts for Target Setting Training

The handouts on the following pages have been set out in a photocopiable format for ease of use. They remain subject to copyright but may be reproduced within the purchasing institution or organization.

HANDOUT 1

Types of target

There should be a combination of types of target, weighted as the manager considers appropriate for the job/individual. The timescales of some targets may be only a few weeks or months if they relate to a specific project or task. At the other extreme some may cover the whole period if appropriate.

Organizational

Separate from the company's business target. It may be possible to identify a target which fits in with an organizational priority eg relating to a customer relationship or implementation of the team briefing initiative.

Departmental

There will be particular issues which will help the efficiency/effectiveness of the department eg relating to:
- improvement of interdepartmental communication;
- improvement of quality/speed of service to other departments;
- budgetary or cost control targets;
- recruitment or training.

Managerial

If the subordinate is a supervisor or manager it may be important to set some targets relating to this aspect of the job eg:
- staff development;
- discipline/control of staff;
- recrutiment/retention.

Technical

Development of technical skills or knowledge or achievement of technical tasks.

Individual

Targets should include at least one aimed at developing the individual. This could mean developing individual skills or improving a particular aspect of the individual's performance.

HANDOUT 2

Target setting for different types of jobs

Most managers could justifiably argue that it is difficult to set targets in their particular department or function. There are certain types of jobs where different approaches may be taken.

Managerial/supervisory

It may be possible to offer more supervisory responsibility than is currently being taken. Consider targets for appropriate aspects of the supervisory role, eg planning, supervision skill, administration, financial, communication.

Routine jobs and services

In some areas of the business the purpose is to provide a service or carry out predetermined tasks without a great deal of scope for discretion by the job holder in what to do or how to do it.

It may be possible to set a few core targets which apply to a number of people and then add a few individual targets with the intention of developing certain team members in a particular direction. If it is not possible to prepare the individual for career advancement it is still important to try to improve how well the job is being done.

In a service function it is always important to strive to improve the service to 'customers'. At more junior levels normally one target will relate to commitment to the job and flexibility.

Creative jobs

It is difficult to set targets which focus on creative aspects of a job because a certain amount of subjectivity prevails at the assessment stage. A key principle is not to set targets which cannot be assessed.

In all jobs certain *individual qualities* will be important and it is possible to set goals against these, eg:

- ability to work effectively with colleagues;
- self-presentation skills;
- relationships with other departments;
- ability to meet deadlines.

If it is important to set targets relating to the *creative* aspect of the job it is essential to agree at the outset how assessment will be made, eg:

- number of times ideas are rejected;
- how well a design is accepted by senior management;
- feedback from customers/clients.

HANDOUT 3

Checklist for setting effective targets

Effective targets should:

- *Be measurable.* This could mean measurable in *quantifiable* terms. If this is not possible then discussion should take place and a record should be made of *standards expected*. There must be an understanding of what constitutes good/poor performance.
- *Include expected completion date or deadline* or agreement on what would be considered good/poor achievement in terms of timescale.
- *Focus on a maximum of six issues.* Identify areas of the job where achievement/improvement will have most impact. Balance organizational, departmental, managerial, technical and individual targets.
- *Be achievable but stretching.* 'Put a 5 foot 10 inch person into 6 feet 3 inches of water, and odds are he'll learn to swim. He may sputter and spit a bit, but he can always hop up off the bottom and get air. Put that same person in 7 feet 4 inches of water, and you may have a dead body on your hands' (Peters, *Thriving on Chaos*, Pan/Macmillan, 1989).
- *Be negotiated and agreed.* Manager and subordinate should prepare separately. Both meet to negotiate and agree targets.
- *Be subject to mid-term modification* by agreement, if external circumstances/conditions change. This does not mean modification of targets should become normal practice. If, however, changes in circumstances are out of the individual's control there could be a case for modification.
- *Entail a two-way commitment.* The manager is committing to assist and provide the necessary resources for targets to be achieved. The subordinate is committing to work towards the targets.

Appendix 2

HANDOUT 4

Methods of measurement and assessment

- Cost
- Speed/deadlines
- Accuracy/number of mistakes
- Evidence of achievement of a task
- Knowledge
- Skill level
- Examples of behaviour change
- Amount of supervision needed

Appendix 3

Example Targets

Managerial targets

Time management
Acquire and develop personal organization skills to improve productivity and performance. Should be able to plan personal and external time and resources to meet the requirements of the job.

Skills and knowledge to be developed by attending an off-job time-management course and subsequent development of time-management techniques and a personal planning diary system.

Success will be measured by ability to prioritize urgent and important work and a decrease in the number of crises occurring over the next six months.

Staff management
Demonstrate staff-management skill by being able to schedule staff to match workload on a weekly basis, taking due care to allocate staff according to experience and expertise as well as providing opportunities for staff development through on- and off-job training.

Schedules of staff loading to be kept and a review of the skills profile of staff to be compared with current status in nine months' time.

Training
Prepare an on-job training package which will help introduce new members of staff to the department by covering issues such as key personnel, working practices, terms and conditions and initial on-job training. Methods should be varied and may include written and verbal material. Publication of the agreed package within the next three months to be followed by a pilot trial over the following three months.

Recruitment
Recruit a sales manager for the sales department by drawing up a job description and personnel specification in discussion with the personnel department. Prepare and implement a plan for attracting a field of candidates; manage the selection process and recruit a suitable candidate by the end of the year. Costs to be monitored with the objective of remaining within budget.

Communications targets

Cross-functional communication
Improve effective communication between the production department and engineering department by establishing regular meetings and developing informal communication methods. Engineering department should be made aware of production problems where they relate to design matters and this will be monitored by seeking a reduction in the number of post-production redesign problems over the next year.

Presentation skills
Develop effective presentation skills by attending the in-company presentations training course and through a programme of structured experience over the coming year which will progressively increase exposure to presentation situations.
   Should be able to deliver customer presentations to company standard without assistance or supervision by the end of the year.

Team briefing
Introduce team briefing to the department and ensure that it becomes a valuable means of facilitating upward and downward communication. Practise team briefing for the department as a model for supervisors to follow and coach supervisors in how to brief their own staff.
   Success will be measured by considering the number and quality of enquiries upwards and by checking that the core brief messages are understood by junior staff after nine months.

Administrative targets

Administrative procedures
Design and agree with the relevant parties a flow diagram of the administrative system which should be adopted for the purchase of equipment and materials. This should take account of current practice and areas for future development or change.

Target Setting

The system should be agreed with the departmental manager within the next two months and then all staff in the department should be briefed on the system. Operation of the system should be continuously monitored and reviewed three months after instigation. Suggestions for further development should then be made. Success will be measured by looking at how workable the system is and whether there is a reduction in the number of supply problems.

Personal computing skills
Become familiar with and competent in the use of the software packages currently used in the department by attendance at an off-job course and through on-job coaching and self development over the next two months.

Should be able to access, set up and manipulate word-processed documents, spreadsheets and databases from raw data without supervision within four months.

Targets for specific functions

Technical skills
Improve technical skills in the field of data communications with the objective of being able to install and maintain new applications packages and to respond effectively to helpdesk enquiries within nine months.

To help in the achievement of this target attendance at relevant seminars and external product promotions will be encouraged as will inclusion on the circulation lists for relevant technical journals.

Finance
Control the annual budgeting and reforecasting process for the company ensuring that adequate instructions are issued to budget holders in a timely fashion so that the company budget can be presented to the board in an acceptable format. Review budget proposals with departmental managers in advance of board agreement and communicate subsequently agreed budgets.

This is to take place for the forthcoming financial year and success will be measured by considering the smooth running and timeliness of the budget preparation and review process.

Personnel
Improve the organization's image in the recruitment market place by providing a quicker response to applicants. The target is to reduce by half the average length of time taken to respond to applicants between:

1 initial application and regret or offer of interview;
2 interview and offer or regret.

This is to be achieved for the forthcoming recruitment round.

Organizational targets

Flexibility

Demonstrate willingness to operate within the organization's objective of achieving flexibility in terms of performance of targets and working times. Should be prepared to carry out a range of different tasks which will vary according to workload and should be prepared to vary working hours to suit workload. When being asked to operate in new areas should be willing to undertake appropriate training. Review progress in nine months' time.

Total quality management

Introduce total quality management concepts and practices to the organization by liaising with external consultants and senior management internally to set up a programme of initial workshops for all employees. This is to be delivered within 12 months. Should enable all senior and middle management to participate in the delivery of workshops to staff in their own areas.

Appendix 4

Reference List of Relevant Videos

Nobody's Perfect, Successful Interviewing Series, Volume 2, BBC Training Videos, 40 minutes.
Illustrates good and bad interviewing techniques including appraisals, information-gathering and disciplinary interviews. Detailed treatment of appraisals, open and closed questions, positive and negative responses and formal and informal interviewing.

Appraisal Skills, Gower, 45 minutes.
Questioning and listening skills in the context of appraisal. Interpretation of action through a 'link' tutor who helps analyse the role plays.

The Appraisal Interview, Melrose, 28 minutes.
Analysis of appraisal skills through the vehicle of a counselling session with the appraiser's manager. Focuses on the relevant skills of performance appraisal interviewing.

How am I Doing?, Video Arts, 26 minutes.
Humorous but ageing video dealing with core appraisal skills using fictitious characters to demonstrate the skills of performance appraisal.

Targeting for Performance, Melrose, 33 minutes.
Scenario of an organization where target setting is being introduced following the principles of SMART (specific, measurable, achievable/agreed, and timebound) targets.

References

Alder, H (1991) 'Seeing is believing: the natural way to success', *Management Decision*, 29(1).
Boyatsis (1982) *The Competent Manager*, Wiley, New York (1990).
Department of Trade and Industry (1992) *The Case for Costing Quality*, DTI, London.
Gallwey, W T (1986a) *The Inner Game of Golf*, Pan, London.
Gallwey, W T (1986b) *The Inner Game of Tennis*, Pan, London.
Garratt, B (1990) *Creating a Learning Organization; a Guide to Leadership, Learning and Development*, Director Books in association with the Institute of Directors, Cambridge.
Handy, C (1981) *Understanding Organizations*, Penguin, Harmondsworth.
Institute of Personnel Management (1992) *Performance Management in the UK, An Analysis of the Issues*, IPM, London.
Kane, J S and Freeman, K A (1986) 'MBO and performance appraisal: a mixture that's not a solution, part 1', *Personnel*, December.
Kane, J S and Freeman, K A (1987) 'MBO and performance appraisal: a mixture that's not a solution, part 2', *Personnel*, February.
Locke, E and Latham, G (1990) *A Theory of Goal Setting and Task Performance*, Prentice Hall, New York.
Lowe, P (1993) *Performance Appraisal*, Kogan Page, London.
McCallum, C (1993) *How to Design and Introduce Appraisal Training*, Kogan Page, London.
Maltz, M (1986) *Psycho-cybernetics*, Simon & Schuster, New York.
Management Charter Initiative (1991) *Crediting Competence, A Guide to APL for Practising Managers*, MCI, London.
Peters, T (1989) *Thriving on Chaos*, Pan in association with Macmillan, London.
Peters, T and Waterman, R (1982) *In Search of Excellence*, Harper & Row, New York.

Rodgers, R and Hunter, J E (1991) 'Impact of management by objectives on organizational productivity', *Journal of Applied Psychology*, April.

Shone, R (1984) *Creative Visualisations*, Thorsons.

Whitlam, Peter J (1993) 'Imagery: its application to goal achievement', paper presented at the International Training and Development Conference, Brussels, and held by IMC Buckingham, England.

Index

acceptable performance 76
administrative functions 51–5, 117–18
    defining targets 55
    individual targets 52–3
    maintenance of standards 51–2
    target examples 117–18
affirmations 108
assessment 21–2
assessment process 68, 115
attitudes 19–20, 70
attraction to like 94
autocratic model 69, 72

Big Brother 20
bonus system 78
bottom-up development 68–9
buyer 57

career development and progression 47, 59
change
    coping with pressures of 19
    and corporate environment 15–17
    secret to introducing 70
communication skills 87–9
    checklist for improving 88
    see also interpersonal skills
communications
    across functions 17, 117
    improving 70
    targets 117
competencies 22, 38–40
    definition 38
    framework of 39
    and individual targets 40
    key roles of management and associated units of 39
    required areas of 39
competency movement 18, 38
confrontation 93–4
continual review 80–81
corporate environment
    and change 15–17
    key trends affecting 15–16
corporate image 19
corporate values 19
creative jobs 113
cross-functional communication 17, 117
cultural norms 70
customer/supplier relationships, personnel assistant role in 54
cynicism 20

decision making in TQM 42–3
delegation 48–9
democratic model 69, 72
departmental targets 111
development programmes 40–41
developmental targets 56–9, 66–7
    success criteria 68

empathy in listening 90–91
employees
    basic needs 24–5
    role of 16
    support needs 16, 20
    traits and behaviours of 27

Target Setting

engineering supervisor 56
exceptional performance 76

feedback 93
finance 118
flexibility 119

generic competencies 38
goal setting 30

halo effect 94
hardware engineer 58
horns effect 94
human needs 16, 20, 24–5, 36
human resource department 22
human resource management, integrated approach 45

inappropriate responses 91
individual targets 112
input and output measurements 28–9
input and output statements 64–5
interim reviews 81
interpersonal skills 86–95, 100
    confrontation 93–4
    empathizing 90–91
    listening techniques 89–90
    questioning 92
    see also communication skills

job description 37

laissez-faire model 69
learning, hands-on or experiential techniques 18
learning organization, concept of 41
listening techniques 89–90

maintenance technician 56
maintenance type activity 78
management by objectives 27–8
    prior introduction of 45
Management Charter Initiative 39
management training 17
managerial jobs 113
managerial targets 112, 116–17
measurement methods 115

meeting arrangements 84
motivation 17–19, 24, 78–9
    and performance appraisal 25–6

National Vocational Qualifications 38
network manager 56
numerical targets 65–6

organizational messages, reinforcing 69–70
organizational targets 111, 119
output statements 64, 65

Pareto principle 77
pay awards 37
perceptual distortions 94–5
performance appraisal 22, 23, 76
    all levels 29
    appropriate positioning of 29
    case study 31–4
        possible answers 109
    forms of 24
    from traits to results-based assessment 27–8
    history and trends 27
    and identification of training needs 26
    implementation aims 24
    interview 25–6, 29
    key aims of 26
    key trends in 30
    negative effects 25–6
    normal reaction to 59
    potential pitfalls of 31–4
    prior introduction of 45
    purpose of 24–7
    quantifying 28
    and target negotiation 28
    targets-based approach 28
    as tool for motivation 25–6
    traits-based approach 28
performance management 23–34
    analysis of issues 30
    definition 30
    key tenet behind 30
    management techniques and approaches relating to 31
    organizations implementing 31
    in relation to target setting 31

Index

performance-related payment systems 37–8
personal computing skills 118
personnel assistant, role in customer/supplier relationships 54
personnel functions 118–19
presentation skills 117
primacy effect 95
problem solving in TQM 42
production targets 49
progress towards targets 21
project supervisor 58–9
promotion 49, 59–60
    unrealistic or undesirable 59
psychology 106, 107

quality circles 44–5
    concept of 44
    integration into daily tasks 44
    potential pitfalls 44
quantitative targets 65–6
questioning 92

rating system 75–6
recency effect 95
recruitment 117, 118
remuneration systems 22, 36–8, 78
resilience 19
review process 68, 74–85
    discussion 21
    ground rules 75
    meetings 84
    preparation 75–7
    rating 75–6
    self-review 80–81
    timescales 81–5
    see also interpersonal skills
reward system 36–8, 78, 79
routine jobs 113

salary review 37, 78, 79
self-fulfilling prophecy concept 106–8
self-review 80–81
senior level interfaces 21
senior management
    target setting 49–51
    training 49–50, 101

training workshops 50–51
sensitivity 19
service functions 51–5, 113
    defining targets 55
    individual targets 52–3
    maintenance of standards 51–2
skills and abilities requirements 16
skills development 48–9, 58–9
skills requirements, *see also* interpersonal skills
staff management 116
stereotypes 94–5
stress relieving 48
success criteria 67–8, 70–73
supervisory jobs 113

target setting
    achievable but stretching 71
    aims of 69–70, 82
    balancing with other responsibilities 77–80
    barriers to 59
    checking and challenging 29
    checklist of requirements 114
    context of 15
    direction and motivation in 18–19
    distinguishing from other responsibilities 85
    examples for different types of jobs 113
    for specific functions 118–19
    ground rules 63, 65, 72
    identifying key areas 69
    implementation 20, 46–7, 50
    individual 40, 41
    integrating with existing systems 35–45
    integrating with other initiatives and systems 22
    introducing 99
    manager's commitment 72
    models of 68–9
    objections to 20, 47, 48, 59
    practicalities of 63–73
    preparation for 46–60
    principle behind 77
    priorities 81
    problems associated with establishing 46
    schematic of process 82
    selection of areas for 77
    senior management 49–51

success factors 46–60
successful implementation 100
technical roles 56–9
timescales 81–5
top-level involvement 19
two-way process 72
see also interpersonal skills
targets 64–5
    examples of 116–19
    types of 111–12
team briefing 117
teamworking 17
technical roles, target setting 56–9
technical skills 118
technical targets 56, 57, 112
time constraints 47–9
time management 116
    techniques 49
    training programme 49
timescales
    from target setting to review 81–5
    recommendation schematic 82
top-down support 68–9
top-level support and involvement 19
total quality management (TQM) 41–5, 76, 119
    causes of failure of implementation 43
    decision making in 42–3
    principles of 42–3
    problem solving in 42–3

trainer roles 19–21, 29, 47–8, 63
training 99–105, 111, 116
    changes in approach to 17–18
    continuous 18
    cost 100
    design of 100
    development of 101
    follow-up and support methods 105
    identification of needs 26, 41
    implementation of 100
    initial skills 17–18
    off-job courses 18, 102–5
    off-the-shelf 101
    offer of 17
    on-site workshop 101–2
    professional 18
    role of competencies in 40
    senior management 49–51, 101
    and target setting skills 82
    workplace 17–18
training programmes 22, 40–41
    core skills of 20

unacceptable performance 76

videos 120
visualization concept 107–8

weighting systems 79–80

p59 Target 1 New knowledge required.
2 New skills to be developed

Develop interpersonal skills with particular emphasis on presentation and influence in meetings. Achieved by attending the company presentation skills training course,
and structured reading
combined with a gradual increase in involvement in team meetings
and ongoing review of development